2.00

DATE DUE

MAR 19 1993	
DEC 2 0 2001	

DEMCO, INC. 38-2931

Essay Index

A NATURALIST OF SOULS

A NATURALIST OF SOULS

Studies in Psychography

BY

GAMALIEL BRADFORD

KENNIKAT PRESS/PORT WASHINGTON, N. Y.

Essay Index

A NATURALIST OF SOULS

Copyright 1926 by Gamaliel Bradford
Reissued in 1969 by Kennikat Press by arrangement with
Houghton Mifflin Company
Library of Congress Catalog Card No: 75-85995
SBN 8046-0543-2

Manufactured by Taylor Publishing Company   Dallas, Texas

ESSAY AND GENERAL LITERATURE INDEX REPRINT SERIES

J'analyse, j'herborise, je suis un naturaliste des esprits.

SAINTE-BEUVE

PREFACE

A Naturalist of Souls was first published in 1917. Since that time the public has become somewhat more interested in psychography, and a study of the origin and development of the art seems likely to make a little wider appeal. I have taken out of the book the chapter on 'The Novel Two Thousand Years Ago' and have inserted in their chronological order chapters on 'Walter Pater,' 'A French Lamb,' and 'A Gentleman of Athens.' Various errors and defects of the earlier edition have also been corrected.

GAMALIEL BRADFORD

WELLESLEY HILLS, MASS., 1925

CONTENTS

A NATURALIST OF SOULS

I
PSYCHOGRAPHY

A NATURALIST OF SOULS

I

PSYCHOGRAPHY

SOME one asked Zola why he used the term 'Naturalism,' when there was nothing about his work that was essentially different from realism or from other literary forms that had been employed for thousands of years before his time. 'I know all that,' he said. 'You are perfectly right. But I needed a name to attract the attention of the public. When I repeat the word over and over, it is bound at last to make people think there is something in it. It is like driving a nail. The first blow does not amount to much; but as you add another, and another, and another, in the end you make progress.'

I confess that my use of the word 'Psychography' was at first something like Zola's use of 'Naturalism.' It was not even my own original invention, though I had coined it for myself before I discovered that it had been used by Professor Saintsbury a few years earlier in discussing the work of Sainte-Beuve. I did not suppose that it

3

meant anything particularly new, but it seemed to sum up processes that have been rather vaguely employed before and to give them a name which might be useful in attracting the attention of the jaded, over-loaded American reader.

I should not now claim that the word meant anything new in substance. All literary and historical methods have been employed over and over again, and the most we can hope to do is to improve and modify them. But the more I practice psychography, the more it seems to me to represent definite phases of literary or biographical production, phases worthy not only of a distinct name, but of careful study.

I can best introduce what I have in mind by making clear one or two things that psychography is not. In the first place, it is not at all properly conveyed or suggested by the word 'portrait.' I have hitherto used this term, because it has the excellent authority of Sainte-Beuve and many others, and because I have not yet found courage to talk about 'psychographs,' and even if I had, publishers and editors have not. But 'portrait' is very unsatisfactory. To carry the terms of one art into another is always misleading, and I have experienced this in the complaint of many critics that as a portrait painter I could present a man at only one moment of his career, that I depicted his character in only one phase, one situation, one set of conditions and circumstances.

Now the aim of psychography is precisely opposite to this. Out of the perpetual flux of actions and circumstances that constitutes a man's whole life, it seeks to extract what is essential, what is permanent and so vitally characteristic. The painter can depict a face and figure only as he sees them at one particular moment, though, in proportion to the depth and power of his art, he can suggest, more or less subtly, the vast complex of influences that have gone to building up that face and figure. The psychographer endeavors to grasp as many particular moments as he can and to give his reader not one but the enduring sum total of them all.

But, it is urged, if the object is thus chronological completeness, in what respect does psychography differ from biography? Simply that biography is bound to present an elaborate sequence of dates, events, and circumstances, of which some are vital to the analysis of the individual subject, but many are merely required to make the narrative complete. From this vast and necessary material of biography, psychography selects only that which is indispensable for its particular purpose, and as the accumulation of books becomes yearly greater and greater, it seems as if this principle of condensation must become more and more pressing in its appeal.

Finally, psychography differs from psychology in that the latter does not deal primarily with individuals, but with general principles, and uses individuals only for the discovery, development, and illustration of those principles.

Psychography, then, is the attempt to portray character, and in discussing psychography we must evidently begin with a clear understanding of what character means. The reader will perhaps pardon my rehearsing the no doubt crude metaphysical analysis which I have found satisfactory for my own purposes. Character is quite distinct from individuality. Individuality, so far as we appear to others in this world, is a vast complex, based primarily upon the body, the material, physical organization, and consisting of all the past history of that organization, its name and all its actions and utterances in their sequence and concatenation with other circumstances and events.

It is, of course, perfectly evident that no words, no possible abstract instruments of thinking, will ever suffice to render this individuality in its completeness. The brush of the painter can at once attain a result that is impossible to language, and although the artist in color never conveys anything like the fullness of individuality, yet the physical portrayal he achieves is to all intents and purposes distinct from the portrayal of any other human being, and so far individual.

, But we poor workers in words have to toil vaguely after a result which is far less conclusive and satisfying. Even the concrete method, employed by the novelist and dramatist, of letting a personage do his own deeds and speak his own words, rarely makes any approach to complete individuality. No single human action, as verbally recorded, can be confined to one human being more than to another, and scarcely any complication of actions. In the same way no word or combination of words is distinctively yours or mine, or Cæsar's or Napoleon's. A thousand women might have murdered Duncan as Lady Macbeth did, and a million men might have said with Hamlet, 'To be or not to be, that is the question.'

Fortunately, in the weltering chaos which is totaled by the word 'individuality,' there is one clue that we can seize, though it is frail and insecure. As we observe the actions of different men, we find that they follow certain comparatively definite lines, which we call habits; that is, the same man will perform over and over again actions, and speak words, which have a basis of resemblance to each other, though the basis is often obscure and elusive. And back of the words and actions we assume from our own experience motives of sensation and emotion, which serve to strengthen and confirm such resemblance. On this vague basis of fact is built the whole fabric of our study and knowledge of our fellow men. The generalization of these habits of action, sometimes expressing itself very obscurely and imperfectly for the acute observer in features and manifestations of the body, constitutes what we call qualities. And the complex of these qualities in turn forms the fleeting and uncertain total which we sum up in the word 'character.' An honest man is one who does honest actions. A simple man is one who does simple actions. An ambitious man does ambitious actions. A cruel man, cruel actions. And so on, almost without limit. The importance of these quality terms is so enormous in our practical daily lives that we are apt, as with many other abstractions, to look upon them as mysterious entities, functions, elements, in some way existing by themselves and entering into the very fiber and substance of the man's inmost soul. And so far as his habits of action are ingrained, vital, rooted deep down in the solid foundations of education and inheritance, these words which express habit are permanent and significant, but their significance comes only from the acts they generalize and the inferred feelings and emotions that prompt those acts, nothing more.

Character, then, is the sum of qualities or generalized habits of action. Psychography is the condensed, essential, artistic presentation of character. And it is now perfectly obvious how frail, how infirm, how utterly unreliable is the material basis upon which psychography rests. First, before we can analyze and generalize a man's habits of speech and action, we must deal with the historical record of that speech and action. And here, of course, we meet the ordinary difficulties in regard to accuracy, which have become so many and so glaring in the light of modern historical research. Most of our knowledge of men's actions in the past depends upon the testimony of others. That testimony, when limited in amount, is extremely uncertain, as shown by the fact that, when abundant, it is usually conflicting. In the small number of cases in which we have the testimony of the man himself, we are apt to be more puzzled and perplexed than when we are without it. As with actions, so with words. It is rare indeed that we can be sure of having even the substance of a man's speech correctly reported to us. Yet for the interpretation of his character it is often of the utmost importance that we should have his exact language, and, if possible, the tone and gesture and emphasis that double or halve its significance.

But these concrete, historical difficulties are but the smallest part of the problem we have to deal with in psychography. Supposing that we have the most reliable record of a man's deeds and utterances, we have advanced but a very little way in establishing the qualities of his character. What actions are just, what actions are generous, what actions are cruel, what actions are foolish? To determine these points requires wide reflection on the bearing of actions in reference to all sorts of conditions and circumstances, and on a man's own judgment and others' judgment of that bearing. The result of such reflection will be different in different minds, and the color that an action assumes to you will be very different from what it assumes to me or to the next critic who considers it.

Further, the generalization of actions is always

imperfect. A man may do one or several kindly actions, yet not have the essential habit of kindliness. A man whose ordinary life runs in the conventional groove of honesty may meet some sudden crisis with an entire reversal of his honest habit. The most minute study, the widest experience in the investigation of human actions and their motives, only make us feel more and more the shifting, terrible uncertainty of the ground under our feet.

The natural question then arises, Of what use is psychography? Why perplex and torment one's self with the study of character, when the difficulty is so great and the result so uncertain, when we seem to begin with nothing and to end with nothing, to be weaving a skein of shadows into a fabric of clouds?

The answer is first, that there is no possible study more fascinating. The problems of character, in others and in ourselves, are teasing us for solution every moment of our lives. The naturalist spends years in studying the life and habits of a bird, or a frog, or a beetle. But every beetle is a beetle, and when you have studied the class, the individual is practically nothing. With the human class every individual is infinitely varied from every other and the field of study is as inexhaustible as it is absorbing.

Moreover, if psychography is an impossible science, it is a necessary one. The psychographer is not a curious dilettante, investigating odd facts to pass an idle hour. The one form of knowledge that is practical above all others is the knowledge of ourselves and of other men. We are all psychographers from the cradle. The child, almost before it can speak, learns just what will affect its father or its mother, and what will not. In our business and in our pleasure, in our hope and in our fear, in our toil and in our repose, we are always considering, examining, calculating upon the action of others. We miscalculate and mistake and blunder disastrously again and again, but we still pursue our instinctive psychography, because it is more important than anything else to the successful conduct and even to the mere living of our lives.

Of course, in the vast chaos of individual action and speech, certain elements are far more significant than others, and it is largely in the discovery and interpretation of these elements that the claim of psychography consists. A man may deliver a formal oration, carefully framed after conventional models, and tell us practically nothing about himself. I long since learned that such material as the fifteen volumes of Sumner's collected works was of little or no value for my purposes. Again, a careless word, spoken with no intention whatever, a mere gesture, the lifting of the hand or the turning of the head, may fling open a wide window into a man's inmost heart.

When one gets to watching for these subtle indications of character, the delight of them is inexpressible. All history and biography are strewn with them, but in astonishingly varying abundance. The Diary of Pepys contains new light on the writer's soul in every page and paragraph. The equally extensive Diary of Madame D'Arblay is artificial, literary, external, and tells comparatively little about Madame D'Arblay herself. General Sherman wears his heart upon his sleeve. Material for depicting him is so plenty that there is only the difficulty of selecting. General Lee conceals himself instinctively behind a barrier of formal reserve, and it is only by long study that one comes across such vivid revelations as his remark at Fredericksburg, 'It is well that this is so terrible, or else we might grow fond of it.'

Of course these revelations of soul are not confined to books or to historical personages. The men and women we meet in casual daily intercourse are always telling — or concealing — the same story of what they are and what they are not. One or two apparently trifling instances have stuck in my memory from their singular significance. A man's wife was caught unexpectedly, in traveling, with little or no money, and obliged to explain her difficulties to the hotel keeper and telegraph to her husband for assistance. The husband sent it at once, but his comment was, 'To think that *my* wife should be stranded in a hotel without money.' Just reflect upon all that little sentence tells of the person who wrote it! Again, I was explaining to a friend a terrible disaster that had happened to another friend and I was myself so agitated and overcome that I could not make anything approaching a lucid story. My hearer was dumbfounded by my condition, and after a moment's effort to gather what I was driving at, his first word was, 'Tell me, at least, does this trouble concern me?' Think of the depths of human nature revealed in that ! Take still another instance. A most worthy, affectionate, devoted husband, who was trying to do all that could be done for an invalid wife, used often to remark, 'When I stand by her grave, I do not wish to have anything to reproach myself with.' Simple, natural words, perhaps, yet they seem to me distinctly significant of a certain type of man.

So, every day, every hour, every minute, we are all of us writing our own psychographs, at any rate piling up ample material for some one else to do it for us.

It is sometimes urged that attention to such minute details in the conduct of historical personages, not to speak of our neighbors, savors of mere gossip. We degrade history and biography, it is said, when we make them depend on careless words and unregarded actions. But if it be true, as I have suggested, that the knowledge of others' characters is absolutely vital to living our own lives and that just such careless words and unregarded actions give us this knowledge of character, then assuredly it is right we should observe them, no matter how trivial and apparently insignificant.

It must be admitted that psychography is always in danger of degenerating into gossip. The difference between the two is simply that gossip springs from the desire to saturate our own emptiness with the lives of others, from a mere idle curiosity about things and persons, bred by an utter lack of interest in ourselves. Gossip makes no distinction of significance between different facts, but gapes wide for all, only more eagerly for those that offer more violent and abnormal distraction. Psychography picks, chooses, and rejects; in a bushel of chaff finds only a grain or two of wheat, but treasures that wheat as precious and invaluable.

Thus far I have spoken of psychography as a science, that is, of the material with which the psychographer deals. Before I touch upon psychography as an art, let me turn for a few moments to the writer from whom I think the psychographer has most to learn, Sainte-Beuve.

It is curious that Sainte-Beuve should have been all his life the most exquisite practitioner of psychography and never have known it. I do not mean that he did not use the word. That is a small matter. But he always thought and spoke of himself as a literary critic, all the while that he was doing work far different from literary criticism.

Indeed, as a mere critic, I do not think that Sainte-Beuve quite deserves the rank usually assigned him. He had little knowledge of any literature besides the classics and his own. Even in speaking of things French, he is a very unsatisfactory guide, outside of the sixteenth, seventeenth, and eighteenth centuries. If he writes of his contemporaries, his judgments, when just, are apt to be intertangled with a personal element of jealousy, which is very unpleasant. Such pure criticism as his study of Theocritus has great and peculiar charm, but it is much less common in his work than is generally supposed.

Where he is really distinguished and original and unrivaled, is as what he himself called, in a rare moment of generalization, 'a naturalist of souls.' In insight into the deep and hidden motives and passions of the soul, in power of distinguishing and defining them, best of all, in cunning and subtle gift of winnowing material so as to select just those significant and telling illustrative words and actions I have spoken of — in all these admirable qualities he had no equal predecessor and has had no follower who can at all approach him. His vast collection of studies of great and striking figures in French history is something quite unmatched in any other literature, and it is coming to stand out more and more and be better appreciated, as it is more widely known. Best of all are his many portraits of women. Madame de Sévigné, Madame de Maintenon, Madame Du Deffand, Madame d'Épinay, and a score of others, representing entirely different aspects of character, are depicted with a fidelity, a sympathy, a delicacy, a just appreciation of mental and moral strength and weakness, which make you feel as if you had known every one of them all your life.

Now it seems evident enough that it is a mere misuse of terms to call such work as this literary criticism. Is it not strange, then, that Sainte-Beuve should never have got really clear with himself about what he was doing, but should have insisted that because these various women wrote letters, therefore, in discussing them, he was discussing literature? The explanation is closely connected with an essential element of his greatness. For he was not an abstract thinker, not a man of theories or formulæ. His attempts to analyze the general character of his work are few, and those that do occur are not lucid or satisfactory. What he did have was an immense, insatiable desire for observation, investigation. Few men have personified more completely than he the spirit of pure scientific curiosity, the love and reverence for the fact in itself, independent of argument, or of any effort to use facts as foundations for theories. One of the ablest of his followers, Scherer, points out that in all Sainte-Beuve's vast work there is little or no repetition. This is true, but Scherer fails to note the significant reason. It is because Sainte-

Beuve adores and imitates the immense individuality of nature. Scherer himself, Brunetière, France, Lemaître, Faguet, Matthew Arnold, all admirers and imitators of Sainte-Beuve, miss his excellence in this point entirely. Not one of them left a quarter part as much work as Sainte-Beuve did. Yet not one of them but in those narrower limits repeats himself over and over in some philosophical discussion or some abstract theory, as all readers will immediately realize in regard to Matthew Arnold. To Sainte-Beuve theories were misleading and unprofitable. Human beings were unlimited in fascination and charm.

Thus, no one was more widely conversant with the material of psychography than he. But there is another phase of psychographic art, which becomes daily of greater interest to me, and which Sainte-Beuve practiced comparatively little. This is the phase of composition. His method of procedure was usually that of simple biography. After a brief introduction, he followed the chronology of his subject, developing different points of character in connection with different circumstances or periods. No doubt great variety can be obtained in this way, as every skilled biographer knows. At the same time, it seems to me that there is a gain in swinging clear from this chronological sequence altogether, and in attaching one's self solely to the presentation of a man's qualities of character, arranged and treated in such logical order as shall give a total impression that will be most effective and most enduring. I confess that I had grave doubts about this procedure at first. I feared that the discussion of qualities in the abstract would be academic, pedagogic, monotonous. Even yet I am not prepared to affirm that this will not prove true and that in the end I shall not have to fall back on simple biographical structure. But my doubt in the matter diminishes daily. Indeed, it is in this regard that the originality and significance of psychography impress me most, and I am astonished to find how rich and varied are the possibilities of artistic presentation with every individual character. Instead of a monotonous renewal of the same qualities in the same order, every individual seems to suggest and to require a different arrangement, a different emphasis. So that I come to feel that Nature herself is the artist and that all one has to do is to lend a patient, earnest ear to her dictation. It is true that not one but a dozen possibilities of composition are indicated in every case and this seems largely to accentuate the uncertainty and unreliability of psychographic art. But, as I have already shown, such wide variety in methods of treatment corresponds to a far wider variety in the material employed, and the search for the best form of developing the material is as delightful as the discovery of the material itself.

After enlarging on Sainte-Beuve especially as the master of all psychographers,[1] I want to refer also to some other artists, to whom I at least owe almost as much. What we may call the quintessence of psychography is those studies of character to be found in the literary and imaginative historians, Tacitus, Clarendon, Saint-Simon, to name no others.

Take Clarendon's character of the Earl of Arundel: 'It cannot be denied that he had in his person, in his aspect, and countenance, the appearance of a great man, which he preserved in his gait and motion. He wore and affected a habit very different from that of the time, such as men had only beheld in the pictures of the most considerable men; all which drew the eyes of most, and the reverence of many, towards him, as the image and representative of the primitive nobility, and native gravity of the nobles, when they had been most venerable;

[1] See Appendix for suggestions for a closer acquaintance with Saint-Beuve.

21

but this was only his outside, his nature and true humor being so much disposed to vulgar delights, which indeed were very despicable and childish. He was never suspected to love anybody, nor to have the least propensity to justice, charity, or compassion, so that though he got all he could, and by all the ways he could, and spent much more than he got or had, he was never known to give anything, nor in all his employments ... never man used or employed by him ever got any fortune under him, nor did ever any man acknowledge any obligation to him. He was rather thought to be without religion than to incline to this or that party of any. He would have been a proper instrument for any tyranny, if he could have found a man tyrant enough to have been advised by him, and had no other affection for the nation or the kingdom, than as he had a great share in it, in which, like the great leviathan, he might sport himself; from which he withdrew himself, as soon as he discerned the repose thereof was like to be disturbed, and died in Italy, under the same doubtful character of religion in which he lived.'

Take again this portrait of the Duke de La Feuillade, by Saint-Simon: 'He had much wit and many sorts of wit. He knew how to impress his merits upon those who saw the surface only, and he had above all the kind of conversation and manners that enchant women. He was delightful to live with, if you cared only for amusement. He was magnificent in everything, liberal, courteous, very brave and very gallant, a great and a daring gamester. He knew well his own good qualities and made parade of them, was self-asserting, always full of moral saws, and loved to argue to show his wit. His ambition was limitless, and as he was inconstant in great and little things both, ambition and the love of pleasure possessed him alternately. He was always eager for reputation, and he had the art of paying apt court to those whose praise could help him and by their praise, which entailed that of others, of making himself a figure in the social world. He appeared to desire friends and sustained the delusion for a long time. He had a heart corrupted to the bottom, a soul of mud, and was an infidel for the fashionable air of being so. In short, he was as thoroughly worthless a man as has been known for years.'

In these wonderful portraits the defects of psychography, which I indicated in beginning, are glaringly apparent, its dependence upon generalizations, usually hasty and never complete, and its consequent unreliability and incapacity for ever being absolute or final. But what light they throw, not only upon the subjects actually presented, but upon the human heart in general, with its passions and weaknesses! It would indeed be vain to hope to equal the vividness, the brevity, the imaginative power of these great masters, but by amplifying their intense concentrated method with fuller detail, with a broader and more elaborate arrangement of design, above all with carefully chosen and significant illustration, the defects of psychography can be partially concealed, if never obliterated. In spite of its defects, or because of them, it is one of the most inexhaustibly fascinating pursuits ever yet discovered to appease the restless activity of the human mind, and the one to which applies most of all the old Roman apothegm,

All longings fail save that to understand.

The reader who has been at all interested in the preceding discussion will, I trust, follow with some curiosity the sequence of the ensuing chapters, which illustrates rather fully at least the practical development of psychography.

In 'Walter Pater,' 'The Poetry of Donne,' and 'A Pessimist Poet' I had no thought of aiming at anything but literary criticism. Yet the psychographical interest and even the beginnings of psychographical method are obvious in both. This is more marked in 'Anthony Trollope,' 'An Odd Sort of Popular Book,' 'Alexander Dumas,' and 'A French Lamb,' though when writing them I had still no thought of psychography as a word or a thing. 'A Great English Portrait Painter' analyzes the work and the character of one to whom psychography is deeply indebted for models and for inspiration. Finally, the last four portraits are elaborate specimens of psychography working consciously, and the last two are as finished psychographs as it is in my power to produce. I trust that others, using a similar method, will produce something much better.

1915

II
WALTER PATER

II

WALTER PATER [1]

So much to read, and so little time to read it! It makes one jealous of every new author, of every new book. With Dante and Shakespeare and Goethe on the shelves — alas, so rarely off them — why do the new books ever tempt us? And yet they do. All of us read them. Many of us read nothing else, and this is surely an abuse. But, after all, Dante and Shakespeare and Goethe are dead, their day is past; and the dead cannot be sufficient for the living. It is one-sided and narrow to forget that past; but it is more one-sided and more narrow to forget the present. That which is modern is ours, and speaks to us as the past, even the past of Pericles, of Elizabeth, never can. So much is true in the abstract; but when it becomes a question of what to read among what is modern, one almost gives it up in despair. The rubbish of a hundred years ago has faded out, so that you do not have to weed an acre to find a flower. But the rubbish of to-day! — it is at least safe to say that there is rubbish, if we name no names.

[1] This discussion of Pater is based upon three of his earlier books, *Renaissance Studies*, *Marius the Epicurean*, and *Imaginary Portraits*.

And even for what is not rubbish tastes are so different. Emerson is not rubbish, nor is Flaubert; yet it is a waste of time for some people to read either. I am very sure it would be equally a waste of time for some people, for very many people, to read the three volumes of Mr. Walter Pater, and I am as sure that there are people who will read them all with infinite delight, and only wish, as I do, that there were three times as many.

I

Mr. Pater's first volume is an attempt to seize and follow, or rather to catch here and there, a definite thread of development in the great spiritual movement of the Renaissance. His preface is important, as giving at the beginning his idea of criticism.

'"To see the object as in itself it really is," has been justly said to be the aim of all true criticism whatever; and in æsthetic criticism the first step towards seeing one's object as it really is, is to know one's own impression as it really is, to discriminate it, to realize it distinctly.'

That will lead in Mr. Pater's work to much fine and close analysis, to a delicate insight.

And again: 'What is important, then, is not that

30

the critic should possess a correct abstract definition of beauty for the intellect, but a certain kind of temperament, the power of being deeply moved by the presence of beautiful objects.' That will give us imagination and sensibility.

Delicate analysis and imaginative sensibility — these Mr. Pater possesses as few have possessed them, these give his work its great, and I must believe its permanent, value. In the eight or ten essays of this early volume these qualities are everywhere apparent. If a fault is to be found, it is with the too great delicacy and subtlety, the over-finish. It is the defect, perhaps, of all Mr. Pater's work: the analysis is so subjective, deals so much with fine points and deeper meanings. It is true that too much abstract theory is dangerous; but the critic must generalize at last. His task should be to detect relations, not only those which are subtle and microscopic, but those which are broader and visible to the general gaze of men if they would open their eyes to see them. He should not stop with the impression things make on himself, but allow just a grain of arbitrariness, and tell us what impression they make on us or ought to make. It is as well that we should have it out with Mr. Pater now, so that we may praise with a clear conscience.

All of his work is a little too fine-spun. Heaven forbid that we should ask for theories of 'vigor and rigor'; but the mind of man is an unstable thing and likes firm ground to rest upon. When we read three volumes word for word — and Mr. Pater's words are too precious to be skipped — we hunger for something which shall savor of conclusions.

But this is fault-finding enough. Let us turn to something pleasanter. One of the first things which strikes one in Mr. Pater's work is its unity of tone. I mean something more than a unity of style, though that, too, is very marked; I mean something almost as distinctive as the indefinable individuality of color which marks some of the great Italian painters, a certain subtle quality hardly to be defined in words. And, indeed, though the application of painters' terms to literature is to be deprecated, color is really the word to apply to what I mean. You feel it before you have read a page in any of these volumes, a tinge of melancholy, of inexplicable sadness, not morbid exactly, certainly not pessimistic, and yet irresistible, leaving an impression for days afterwards. Mr. Pater has described this himself better than I can. It makes one think of his Watteau: 'A seeker after something in the world, that is there in no satisfying measure, or not at all.'

But I must say a few words of the 'Renaissance Studies' before we come to 'Marius.' Certainly the most charming of them, the most sensitive and delicate, is that on Leonardo, and in it the Mona Lisa: 'She is older than the rocks among which she sits; like the vampire she has been dead many times and learned the secrets of the grave; and has been a diver in deep seas, and keeps their fallen day about her; and trafficked for strange webs with Eastern merchants; and as Leda was the mother of Helen of Troy, and, as Saint Anne, the mother of Mary; and all this has been to her but as the sound of lyres and flutes, and lives only in the delicacy with which it has moulded the changing lineaments and tinged the eyelids and the hands.'

The long essay on Winckelmann has much that is deep and true about the Greek world and its relation to us moderns. And the conclusion is especially noticeable because it gives us the clearest and most definite statement we can obtain in regard to Mr. Pater's theory of life.

'Well, we are all *condamnés*, as Victor Hugo says: "*Les hommes sont tous condamnés à mort avec des sursis indefinis*"; we have an interval and then our place knows us no more. Some spend this interval in listlessness, some in high passions, the wisest in

art and song. For our one chance is in expanding
that interval, in getting as many pulsations as possible into the given time. High passions give this
quickened sense of life, ecstasy and sorrow of love,
political or religious enthusiasm or the enthusiasm
of humanity. Only be sure it is passion, that it does
yield you this fruit of a quickened, multiplied consciousness. Of this wisdom, the poetic passion, the
desire of beauty, the love of art for art's sake has
most; for art comes to you professing frankly to
give nothing but the highest quality to your moments as they pass and that simply for those
moments' sake.'

We shall find this theory of life again in 'Marius,'
the younger Marius, for the later Marius passes
out of it and beyond it apparently, or at least
modifies it to a great degree. Whether Marius and
Mr. Pater are one and the same, I do not know.
But the theory is not altogether a new one. It was
Goethe's, as Mr. Pater himself points out. It has
been and is that of some very lovely souls, not only
of those who own it, but of many who follow it unconsciously, opening their lives daily and hourly to
the sweet influences of the world. But — oh, there
is another side! Think of the small number to
whom such a path is open. 'All spiritual progress

is confined to a few,' says Mr. Pater himself. But
the many, the many, to whom culture is an un-
heard-of, far-off, impossible thing! The many who
toil and suffer and curse day by day an unbeauti-
ful, unlovable world! Must there not be some place
for them, too, in one's scheme of things? Shut them
out as you can, they will break in. Your sweet,
passionate world-dream will be marred if human
woe can mar it. Sénancour has said it: 'How can a
life be happy passed in the midst of those who
suffer?'

II

We are just beginning to learn how near the
later Roman world is to us, and how much it has to
teach us. Read M. Gaston Boissier's 'Religion Romaine' and his 'Opposition sous les Césars.' Read
M. Constant Martha's 'Moralistes sous l'Empire
Romaine.' Read Pliny's 'Letters,' and, above all,
the 'Thoughts' of Marcus Aurelius. It surprises
one to see so much of what we think and feel anticipated there to the very life. That is what gives
its interest to the story of 'Marius the Epicurean,' and one should read it, as Mr. Pater has
evidently written it, with such books ready to
one's hand. For 'Marius' is not a novel, at least

not what we commonly understand by that name.
Doubtless many people have avoided it, as I did,
fearing some 'Zenobia, Queen of Palmyra,' or some
'Last Days of Pompeii'; for certainly no one has
yet succeeded in reproducing in fiction the manners of antiquity without pedantry and affectation.
Even Mr. Pater has here and there a touch which
recalls the 'Last Days'; 'The neat head projecting
from the collar of his gray *pænula* or traveling
cloak.' That sort of thing is what jars in Bulwer's
novel. But in 'Marius' such things sink and are
lost. What is profound and thoughtful in it out-
weighs and hides them wholly. Yet, as I said,
'Marius' is not a novel, and whoever reads it as
one will be disappointed. It has no plot, no climax,
and only one character. It is, in short, what its
second title calls it: 'The Sensations and Ideas of
Marius the Epicurean.' But, if I dare whisper it,
it will be even more interesting, read as the sensations and ideas, not of an Epicurean seventeen
hundred years ago, but now, to-day, and here.
Whether one should still call him Marius or not, I
cannot tell.

We see the young Marius first living in his 'old
country-house, half-farm, half-villa,' his father
dead, growing up with the country sights and

sounds around him, still, as a boy, tenderly and seriously alive to the ceremonies of the religion of his ancestors. There is many a lovely picture here of that youthful life and its surroundings, more lovely in contrast with the perturbed world which meets us later. Here, as so often afterwards, does not many a one among us see himself? And then that strange journey to the temple of Æsculapius with its healing dreams and the sweet Greek legend of the god's children: '"But being made like to the immortal gods, they began to pass about through the world, changed thus far from their first form that they appear eternally young, as many persons have seen them in many places — ministers and heralds of their father, passing to and fro over the earth, like gliding stars."'

But, alas, these childish days cannot last forever. Would they could! And next it is the youth who in his new hopes and aspirations comes before us. It is art now and beauty, which has replaced the old, traditional piety, art, or, more properly, the artist, personified in Flavian. For one cannot but treat all these characters as personifications, they so evidently appear and disappear only to fill a place in Marius's life. With this new companion much is learned and much forgotten. They imbibe together the richness of this new phase of the world.

But we must hurry on, past the lovely dream of 'Cupid and Psyche,' past the death of Flavian. Life begins to look more serious now, and this outward loss and deprivation drive the thought of Marius within. It is delicately conceived that the death of his beloved friend and helper should not make him feel more strongly the reality of a future world, as happens so often with commoner, or rather more emotional, natures. Precisely this union of intellectual probity with the finest sensibility is what gives the character its charm; for there are others who have seen the tomb close over all they loved, and yet have felt bound to trust their passion less and their reason all the more, in spite of the heart's cry, 'We must press those lips again.' It is this subtlety, everywhere present, which cuts off Mr. Pater from a widespread popularity, and will make him all the nearer to the few for whom he writes. But Marius in the meanwhile doubts and questions and reasons until he comes to his Epicureanism proper, his clear and settled, and, as it seems to him, final view of life: the real Epicureanism of Epicurus, that is to say, a complete intellectual skepticism, a resolution to make the

most of life simply as it is, day by day, coupled —
and here is the essential limitation — with the
finest and most delicate moral nature in the holder
of the theory. Mr. Pater has shown excellently the
nature of this true Epicureanism, with a perfect
consciousness that it is an anomaly; for the theory,
in its very essence, requires to be modified by what
it denies, a belief in the ideal, else it leads quickly to
unalloyed hedonism. This Marius finds out as he
goes on; but, for the present, life and sensation, not
coarse, not animal sensation, but the joy and delight
of beauty in every form, calm him, satisfy him. He
has formulated his mystical religion of the eye: that
which is vulgar and disgusting and repulsive to the
eye must be rejected, must be wrong. And this is a
religion of Mr. Pater's own, as every one must feel
who notices how, again and again, he judges everything by color, judges and describes everything by
delicate degrees of light.

And now comes Rome, "'The most religious city
in the world.'" Marius goes thither, ostensibly
that he may fill some office near the person of the
Emperor; but evidently because his experience requires it. And after this his intellectual progress is a
little difficult to trace. It seems as if, from the first,
he had almost unconsciously felt a flaw in this new

principle of his, and now it cannot quite satisfy him in the presence of men and of the moving world. The Emperor himself, so like him in some respects, stands to Marius in many things as an example of what he ought to avoid. How? It would be hard to say. The question now is not one of theories for the intellect, but of a new mode of action, a new way of taking life. And it is here that Marius comes across the strange light which had just dawned upon the Roman world. The character through which this light first comes to him, Cornelius, is somewhat vague. Like Flavian, he stands for a type, a side of the ideal which Marius requires and has not found. In himself he is not likely to interest or detain the reader. By his means Marius, as I said, is brought in contact with Christianity, and the most masterly part of the book is the treatment of the effect of this contact on his mind. It is not an intellectual effect. Never, I think, is the intellectual side of Christianity considered or discussed, nor does Marius ever wholly resign his original Cyrenaicism, his reliance on the guidance of the eye. But his old theory, his Epicureanism, was narrow, limited, cold; it needed largeness and humanity. We must, indeed, stand intellectually isolated, alone. The sweet ideal can have no assured value out of ourselves. It is foolish to deny it, foolish to mourn for it, and yet — Something must be heard besides logic, something must be allowed to sweeten, to soften this hard, cold Roman world. Can Epicureanism do it? Never. Can Stoicism do it? Hardly; for the sweetest of Stoics sat at the gladiatorial spectacle, impassible through all the hours, for the most part, indeed, actually averting his eyes from the show, reading, or writing on matters of public business; yet, after all, indifferent. He was revolving, perhaps, that old Stoic paradox of the *imperceptibility of pain*. Paradox, indeed; and a paradox somewhat cruel and mocking for the generality of men who are not Stoics, and to whom pain is not imperceptible, but very real, perhaps the most real thing in all this world. '*Sunt lacrimæ rerum.*' That is what Epicurus never knew. That is what Marius had never found in all his Cyrenaicism; that was what he must find, so that at times it seemed to him as if the world had nothing else worth seeking.

'We are constructed for suffering!' he writes in his journal. 'What proofs of it does one day afford, if we care to note them, as we go — a whole long chaplet of sorrowful mysteries.' Somewhat different from the tone of 'Cupid and Psyche' and the dreams of Flavian!

Here it is that Marius meets the spirit of Christianity then abroad in the world. The gospel of the sick and poor found him, too, in the calm, pure faces of its worshipers, in their *other-worldliness*, their superhuman joy. It found him in the white-robed children, in the strong, free music of their hymns. It found him, more than all, in that touching letter from the churches of Lyons and Vienna with all its sacrifices, with all its pain: 'Last of all, the blessed Blandina herself, as a mother that had given life to her children, and sent them like conquerors to the great king, hastened to them, with joy at the end, as to a marriage feast; the enemy himself confessing that no woman had ever borne pain so manifold and great as hers.' It was this spirit, not Cyrenaicism, Marius felt, which would regenerate the world. And yet he himself stands to the end outside of it. It touches him much and teaches him more; it has not won him. The old tyrannical intellect still stands behind and draws him back. The world is regenerated for others, not for him. Oh, the pity of it, the infinite pity of it! That no one has ever come to heal this miserable war! That is what gives the book its sadness. Not that Marius has not his sacrifice also; for this opening of his heart bears fruit with him, too, in its way, and he tells himself that, perhaps after all, one's highest gain, one's highest emotion, even from the Epicurean point of view, is to be found in that love which lays down its life for its friend. It is in this way that when he and Cornelius are captured as Christians, he remains in bonds himself and sets Cornelius free, knowing that perhaps death will be the result. But the sacrifice has no religious after-sweetness, a bitterness rather, and a hopeless wish that all sacrifice were unnecessary. 'Had there been one to listen just then, there would have come, from the very depth of his desolation, an eloquent utterance at last, on the irony of men's fates, on the singular accidents of life and death.' All this had happened far from Rome, and the prisoners must be carried thither for trial. But the journey was too severe. Marius's strength failed, and the guards left him in a little hut by the roadside to await the end. It comes at last, not altogether bitterly, though still sadly. If the light had not dawned for him, at least he felt that a new day was breaking on the world. And the Christian souls about him watched his fading life with tenderness.

'In the moments of his extreme helplessness their mystic bread had been placed, had descended like a snowflake from the sky, between his lips. Gentle fingers had applied to hands and feet, to all those old passageways of the senses, through which the world had come and gone from him, now so dim and obstructed, a medicinable oil. It was the same people who, in the gray, austere evening of that day, took up his remains and buried them secretly, with their accustomed prayers; but with joy also, holding his death, according to their generous view in this matter, to have been of the nature of a martyrdom; and martyrdom, as the Church had always said, a kind of sacrament with plenary grace.'

Yet, after all, the conclusions one gets from this life of Marius are not quite definite enough. It is the same complaint we made in the beginning. It will be said that you cannot sum up a man's life in any single formula. So many moods, so many impulses, cannot be reduced to one impression of any sort whatever. Certainly; and yet almost every one's inward life, given the circumstances which have moulded it, stands before you in a sort of wholeness. Now, to me at least that of Marius does not. I cannot feel that Mr. Pater is always quite clear about the character he has in hand, and the chief figure seems to share a little in the vagueness of the lesser forms which surround him. Yet the very subtlety of analysis which causes this vagueness has its value. Perhaps bolder strokes and more dramatic treatment were inconsistent with the peculiar fineness which gives the book its charm.

I have said nothing yet of Mr. Pater's style, because it is everywhere evident that his style is subordinate to his matter. I do not mean by that that he has no thought of style. Everything he has written shows the contrary. But his style follows the thought, and takes form from it; he is not of the school which studies phrases for their own sake. Yet, in spite of this, in spite of the subtlety and delicacy of the ideas, I sometimes think that his greatest charm lies in expression. It would be a curious thing to point out the change which has come about from the best English style of the last century to that of this, a change as great, if not greater, than that from the style of the Elizabethans to the style of the last century. Take any of Dryden's great prefaces, for instance, or Swift, at his best, and compare it with some pages of Ruskin or Hawthorne. And the same is true in French of the change from Voltaire to Chateaubriand. Some people will prefer one and some the other; though a catholic taste will find the best specimens of either each perfect in its own way. Only you must be sure to have the best, and it would be hard to find better examples of the modern style than can be taken from Mr. Pater. It is not that his style is without defects. It unquestionably lacks vigor and distinctness, unquestionably lacks power, as the best modern styles too often do. More than that, it is frequently careless, or appears so, in the unpleasant repetition of words; for instance: 'And on the crown of the head of the David there remains a morsel of *unhewn* stone, as if by one touch to maintain its connection with the place from which it was *hewn*.' This is very common with Mr. Pater, and certainly might be avoided: a slight thing, but a very annoying one. And, further, in his effort to obtain new and delicate effects, he sometimes uses words which are new and over-delicate: 'The worshiper was to recommend himself to the Gods by becoming fleet and serpenting and white and red like them.' I am not quite sure what 'serpenting' means, but I am very sure that the word is somewhat beyond the limits of perfect Atticism, and one finds other cases of the same sort.

But this is not an occasion for fault-finding. A style like Mr. Pater's ought to be taken in thankfulness, without too much questioning, and only a prayer for more of the same kind. For what richness it has, and what sweetness always! Every word has its meaning with him, and its value, and even the last defect I mentioned comes from an effort to charge words with more meaning than they can bear:

'The sense of a certain delicate *blandness*, which he relished, above all, on returning to the chapel of his mother, after long days of open-air exercise, in winter or stormy summer.' The word will hardly hold all the vague emotion which is forced into it.

And the descriptions! I have already spoken of the Mona Lisa in the 'Renaissance Studies,' but 'Marius' is full of such things. Mr. Pater's rendering of nature has not passion. Passion, in any form, is not frequent in his writing. But all his description has such infinite delicacy, such sensibility to form, to movement, to color! And his wonderfully skillful use of words comes in to help him. Everywhere he has phrases which give nature a new meaning, as subtly as ever Shelley: 'Firm, golden weather,' 'Days brown with the first rains of autumn,' 'And yet so quiet and wind-swept was the place,' 'Dun coolness,' 'It was the very presentment of a land of hope; its hollows brimful of the shadow of blue flowers.' And he has longer descriptions, all touched with the same enchantment. Take one among so many.

'The orchard or meadow, through which their path lay, was already gray in the dewy twilight, though the western sky, in which the greater stars were visible, was still afloat with ruddy splendor, seeming to repress by contrast the coloring of all earthly things, yet with the sense of a great richness lingering in their shadows. Just then the voices of the singers, "a voice of joy and health," concentrated themselves, with a solemn antistrophic movement, into an evening, or "candle" hymn, *the hymn of the kindling of the lamp*. It was like the evening itself, its hopes and fears, and the stars shining in the midst of it, made audible. Half above, half below the level mist, which seemed to divide light from darkness (the great wildflowers of the meadow just distinguishable around her skirts, as she moved across the grass), came now the mistress of the place, the wealthy Roman matron, left early a widow by the confessor Cæcilius, a few years before.'

But by far the most remarkable piece of style in 'Marius' is the discourse delivered by the Emperor Marcus Aurelius, after his triumph, to the assembled Roman people. Dramatically considered, it is, perhaps, a little out of character. Though we know that Aurelius did sometimes exchange the Emperor's throne for the philosopher's chair, it is hardly to be supposed that in the midst of the conventional solemnity of a great public festival he would deliver such a very philosophical discourse as this, a discourse which the vulgar would hardly have heard without a yawn. But, setting this point aside, and we can well afford to do it, the discourse remains a wonderful piece of work. Of course little, if any, of it, is original. It is pieced together from the Emperor's 'Thoughts,' a fragment here and a fragment there; but the piecing is so skillfully done that it makes a far more consistent whole than the 'Thoughts' themselves. And the style, though delicate as everywhere else in the book, is stronger than is usual with Mr. Pater. Take the very first sentence.

Collier translates: 'Examine the size of people's sense, and the condition of their understandings, and you'll never be fond of popularity or afraid of censure.'

Mr. Long translates: 'Penetrate inward into men's leading principles, and thou wilt see what judges thou art afraid of, and what kind of judges they are of themselves.'

49

Mr. Pater's paraphrase runs thus: 'Art thou in love with men's praises, get thee into the very soul of them, and see! — see what judges they be, even in those matters which concern themselves.'

What a difference! And there is the same difference all through. Certainly such a rendering may be called a translation in the fullest sense of the word, and those who would know Marcus Aurelius in future must study him here. I wish I could quote it all. In so much richness it is hard to choose.

'How soon may those who shout my name to-day begin to revile it, because glory, and the memory of men, and all things beside, are but vanity — a sand-heap under the senseless wind, the barking of dogs, the quarreling of children weeping incontinently upon their laughter.'

'I find that all things are now as they were in the days of our buried ancestors — all things sordid in their elements, trite by long usage, and yet ephemeral. How ridiculous, then, how like a countryman in town, is he who wonders at aught. Doth the sameness, the repetition of the public shows weary thee? Even so doth that likeness of events make the spectacle of the world a vapid one. And so it must be with thee till the end. For the wheel of the world hath ever the same motion, upward and downward, from generation to generation. When, when shall time give place to eternity?'

I said the true Marcus Aurelius was to be found here; but has not that cry something of a pain which the Emperor never knew? Is it not rather the voice of Marius himself?

III

If 'The Renaissance' is the root, and 'Marius' the stem, the 'Imaginary Portraits' are the flower. In these Mr. Pater's critical insight and his imaginative sensibility melted together have produced the most delicate work he has ever done. They are not all equal, however. To take the last first, the sketch of 'Duke Carl of Rosenmold,' seems to me the least satisfactory of the four. It stands, perhaps, for the ideal Goethe; but the ideal Goethe could never have been very human, and Duke Carl, in spite of his light and joyousness, is a little vague, a little in the air. Much less so is the first 'Portrait,' that of a 'Prince of Court Painters.' The life and development of Watteau are sketched by the hand which drew Marius, with the same grace, the same sweetness, the same delicate sadness brooding over all. Only here, Mr. Pater has, I think unfortunately, adopted a dramatic form, or I should say, an objective form, in that his study is made, not in his own person, but in that of a lady who knew Watteau and loved him. I say 'unfortunately,' because in the actual representation of character Mr. Pater is not strong. This is shown by the fact that in the whole four hundred and fifty pages of 'Marius' there is not a single conversation, setting aside translations, except the few words exchanged at the death-bed of Flavian, and this, too, when often, as when Marius visits the Emperor and his family, it seems as if conversation would surely be the simplest way of developing the story. The 'Prince of Court Painters' shows Mr. Pater's weakness in this direction even more strongly. It is true that he does occasionally remember what he has undertaken and give a little dramatic touch as, in the journal, where Watteau's painting of another woman is alluded to; but constantly he speaks as no woman in those times could have spoken, and alludes to things which must have been beyond her ken. You never feel that it is really any one but himself. One's mind is quickly made up to this, however, and then everything is forgotten but the exquisite workmanship. What a description is this:

'The sullenness of a long wet day is yielding just

now to an outburst of watery sunset, which strikes from the far horizon of this quiet world of ours, over fields and willow woods, upon the shifty weather-vanes and long-pointed windows of the tower on the square — from which the Angelus is sounding — with a momentary promise of a fine night.'

Have we not seen it all of us, here as well as in Valenciennes, the long light over the willows on the shifty weather-vanes and the melancholy Angelus sounding?

If I have ventured to find fault with the first portrait and the last, it is only because the other two are perfect, each in its kind. 'Denys l'Auxerrois' has perhaps no one passage which stands much above the rest, or beyond other parts of Mr. Pater's writing; but it is conceived and developed in the most exquisite unity and harmony with hardly a weak point anywhere. It is the same old mediæval France which Mr. Pater dwelt on in his essay on 'Aucassin and Nicolette,' that strange middle age with its wild fancies, its grotesque passions, its childish glee, and, above all, its inexplicable sadness, forever brooding over something it cannot understand, over a past too deep for it, over a future which hangs unfathomably far away. But

Auxerre! 'Its most characteristic atmosphere is to be seen when the tide of light and distant cloud is traveling quickly over it, when rain is not far off, and every touch of art or time on its old building is defined in clear gray.' And Denys himself, when he stirs and startles Dean and Canon and Prebendary in that mad game of ball, and when he turns Auxerre upside down with his strange, half-animal fascination. And the madness which took possession of them: 'Heads flung back in ecstasy — the morning sleep among the vines, when the fatigue of night was over — dew-drenched garments — the serf lying at his ease at last.' It is the old Greek Bacchanalia, but still with the touch of sadness in it, not wild, not free, not spontaneous, not child-like any longer. And Denys as he works in his quiet refuge among the monks — Denys as he frames his organ, as he wanders in irresistible frenzy out into the world again, narrowly escaping from his enemies by plunging into the stream. 'Some indeed fancied they had seen him emerge again safely on the deck of one of the great boats loaded with grapes and wreathed triumphantly with flowers.' Last of all, Denys, with a wild longing for the old enthusiasm, the old adoration, making his way among the crowd at the festival, rousing the passion of the mob, torn limb from limb, so that 'the monk Hermes sought in vain next day for any remains of the body of his friend. Only, at nightfall, the heart of Denys was brought to him by a stranger, still entire.' Is not this, all, one of those stone dreams which has stolen down some midsummer night from a cathedral portal to bewitch us? A sweet bewilderment of lutes and pipes and cymbals, a wild cry, a flash of light, and it is gone.

Sebastian Van Storck is deeply contrasted with the preceding, and shows Mr. Pater in a different and stronger vein. Instead of Auxerre and mediæval France, we are in Holland, in Holland which seems modern even as it was two hundred years ago. And yet here, too, is something of the same sadness, the same shade, but clearer and colder as the northern climate would, in its nature, be. And the main subject is as cold as the general treatment. Strange picture, this intoxicated idealism, this Spinozism run mad! Is it not fascinating, absorbing, the story of this youth who with the charm of life around him, grows colder and colder, shuts himself into his cabinet where he could 'yield himself, with the only sort of love he had ever felt, to the supremacy of his difficult thoughts.

A kind of empty place,' where 'of living creatures only the birds came there freely.' And as he goes on everything human falls more and more away from him. Art falls, a trouble, a mere disturbance of the divine peace, after all. Love falls, the woman was not worthy of him. To his mother who reproaches him, 'She must needs feel, a little icily, the emptiness of hope, and more than the due measure of cold in things for a woman of her age, in the person of a son who desired but to fade out of the world like a breath,' he answers, '"Good mother, there are duties towards the intellect also, which women can but rarely understand."' Last of all fades the enthusiasm of the idea itself. The one eternal substance, all-thinking, all-enfolding, inspires love no longer, but indifference only. 'And at length this dark fanaticism, losing the support of his pride in the mere novelty of a reasoning so hard and dry, turned round upon him, as our fanaticism will, in black melancholy.' And the end comes. But, as in the case of Marius, sacrifice softens the harshness of it, makes it pardonable. 'Only, when the body of Sebastian was found, apparently not long after death, a child lay asleep, swaddled warmly in his heavy furs, in an upper room of the old tower, to which the tide was almost risen; though the building still stood firmly, and still with the means of life in plenty. And it was in the saving of this child, with a great effort, as certain circumstances seemed to indicate, that Sebastian had lost his life.'

IV

If I have said half of what I feel, I have shown those who would care for Mr. Pater's writing that they would care for it very much indeed. It is easy to praise it vaguely, but nothing can render its infinite grace and indescribable charm. You must go to the books themselves. Read them in their natural order: the 'Renaissance Studies,' then 'Marius,' then the 'Portraits.' If you like one, you will certainly like all. If you do not like the first, you will hardly care for the others.

I do not know whether it is worth while to insist upon the limitations to all this. I have indicated them. Mr. Pater has not dramatic power, the power of presenting characters. Neither is he a writer to go to for intellectual or moral support. Certain people might find these in him; but most of us would not. Nor is he an artist of the highest order, in spite of his style; he has not the broad, swift, unerring touch of the great masters. I have said that his description had not passion. I mean by that, that in spite of delicate shades and subtle insight, he never could write such things as Keats's 'Nightingale':

> 'Now more than ever seems it rich to die,
>   To cease upon the midnight with no pain,
>   While thou art pouring forth thy soul abroad
>   In such an ecstasy!
>   Still wouldst thou sing, and I have ears in vain —
>   To thy high requiem become a sod.'

Or this, in another strain, of Obermann:

'La paix d'un lieu semblable n'est qu'un abandon momentané, sa solitude n'est point assez sauvage. Il faut à cet abandon un ciel pur du soir, un ciel incertain mais calme d'automne, le soleil de dix heures entre les brouillards.'

An intensity of this high order Mr. Pater has not, either in his description of nature or of human life. And there is one thing more. This melancholy, this sadness, which haunts all his writing, is it quite healthy, quite sound? After 'Marius,' and even more, after 'Denys' and 'Sebastian,' does not one need a breath of this fresh, cold, winter air? Because the melancholy is so seductive, it is all the more dangerous.

But it would be ungracious to complain, or even to remember these things, when so much is given us. I see Mr. Pater's admirers already branding me as a traitor, and I would let no one be more enthusiastic than myself. After all, the broad, all-embracing artists are more praised, more admired; but are they so much treasured as those who turn only to a few, singing to them secretly the music they best love to hear?

1888

III
THE POETRY OF DONNE

III
THE POETRY OF DONNE[1]

POETS of the first rank may be expected to unite the praises of all schools of critics. Those of a lower order, those, at any rate, who are read only by the few, have generally a faction that adores them and another that rejects them wholly. This is more or less the case with Shelley, with Leopardi, with Browning. It is at present the fortune of Donne to be ignored by the general public, and to be at the same time an object of enthusiasm to very different minds among those who know. This will be sufficiently proved by two quotations. One is from Lowell: 'What are the conditions of permanence? Immediate or contemporaneous recognition is not one of them, or Cowley would be popular. . . . Nor can mere originality assure the interest of posterity, else why are Chaucer and Gray familiar, while Donne, one of the subtlest and most self-irradiating minds that ever sought an outlet in verse, is known only to the few?' The other is from a critic whose

[1] Since this essay was written, much study, both biographical and editorial, has been given to Donne; but it has not changed the essential character of the man or the splendor of his poetry.

taste and judgments are certainly quite different from Lowell's, Swinburne, who, in his rhetorical fashion, refers thus to Donne, while speaking of the prose writings of Ben Jonson: 'That chance is the ruler of the world I should be sorry to believe and reluctant to affirm; but it would be difficult for any competent and careful student to maintain that chance is not the ruler of the world of letters. Gray's Odes are still, I suppose, familiar to thousands who know nothing of Donne's Anniversaries; and Bacon's Essays are conventionally if not actually familiar to thousands who know nothing of Ben Jonson's Discoveries. And yet it is certain that in fervor of inspiration and depth and force and glow of thought and emotion and expression Donne's verses are as far above Gray's as Jonson's notes or observations on men and morals, on principles and on facts, are superior to Bacon's in truth of insight, in breadth of view, in vigor of reflection, and in concision of eloquence.' It will be noticed that both writers emphasize the merit of Donne by a comparison with Gray.

Donne's reputation among men of letters has not always been so high. Dr. Johnson selected him as the type of what was objectionable in the so-called metaphysical poets, and he was certainly repugnant enough to the taste of the eighteenth century. But among his own contemporaries he was regarded with enthusiasm both as a poet and as a man. Ben Jonson, no easy judge, called him 'the first poet of the world in some things': and Carew, in his admirable eulogy, speaks of him as

> 'A king who ruled as he thought fit
> The universal monarchy of wit.'

We shall find, I think, that the study of his poems fully justifies this high estimate of him, though his unpopularity with those who read to pass an idle hour is perfectly explicable.

I

Our materials for the life of Donne are more abundant than is the case with many Elizabethan writers. Besides the charming narrative of Walton, there are biographical facts contained in Donne's own poems; above all, a great number of his letters are extant, affording valuable information, especially as to his later years. What would we not give for such precious documents from the hand of Shakespeare!

John Donne was born in London in the year 1573. The most interesting thing we know about his youth is that his parents were strongly Roman

Catholic, and made every effort to bring him up in that religion. He was sent to the University of Oxford in his twelfth year that he might avoid the oath, which was not administered to those under sixteen, and which, as a Catholic, he could not take. According to Walton, he left Oxford for Cambridge, and completed his education there; but this statement is said to be unfounded. Walton also tells us that in the seventeenth year of his age he was admitted to Lincoln's Inn, and there began the study of law. What is more important, from the light it throws on his character, is the statement that soon after this he entered into an examination of the Catholic and Protestant creeds, pursuing his researches through the gloomiest depths of theological controversy. Nothing could be more like Donne. The word which stamps itself on every line of his works, on every trait of his nature, is 'intensity,' that restless, hungry energy of mind, which will not let a man shut his eyes while there is a corner of thought unprobed, unlightened. Vigor of intellect, fervor of emotion — these are what give Donne his high position as a man and as a poet.

So far as we can judge from the many poems that he wrote about this time, his theological studies were followed by a plunge into dissipations of a quite untheological nature. Here, too, intensity is still the word. No depth of passion — let us speak frankly, sensuality — was too much for this eager temper, this fierce and energetic soul.

In the year 1596, Donne appears to have gone with the Earl of Essex on the expedition to Cadiz. When he returned he was made secretary to the Lord Keeper Elsmore, and through him became acquainted with Lady Elsmore's niece, whom he afterwards married. The history of the match is curious. Sir George Moore, the lady's father, being informed of Donne's attachment to his daughter, opposed it, not unnaturally, as she was but sixteen, and Donne's prospects were not over-brilliant. The young people were constant to each other, and were at length secretly married. Sir George was indignant and took the short-sighted step of getting Donne dismissed from his place. When Donne heard of this, he wrote his wife with the characteristic signature, 'John Donne, Ann Donne, un-done,' to appreciate which it is necessary to remember that the proper name was then pronounced like the participle. Sir George even went further, and managed to have Donne and two of his friends committed to prison. The confinement was short, and father and son-in-law were finally reconciled;

but Donne was not out of his difficulties. Sir George, repenting of his hasty severity, made an attempt to have the ex-secretary reinstated. In this he was unsuccessful, and as he refused to help support the young couple, their position was a hard one. At this time both circumstances and inclination led Donne toward the Church; but conscientious scruples and the memory of his past life deterred him. For a number of years he struggled on, assisted by his friends. His reputation as a scholar and a wit grew constantly, and in the year 1610 he wrote, at the request of the King, his book against the Catholics, entitled 'Pseudo-Martyr.' The next year he was abroad for some time with one of his patrons, Sir Robert Drury. After his return he began to have a hope of secular preferment about the Court; and this was probably the cause of his connection with the infamous Carr, afterwards Earl of Somerset. We have a number of his letters to Carr, and also his 'Epithalamium,' composed for the marriage of Somerset and the divorced Countess of Essex. His expectations, if he had any, were, however, disappointed by the exposure and condemnation of that well-matched pair.

Some record of Donne's existence in the unhappy years after his marriage is preserved for us in his letters, which impress one chiefly by a tone of manly dignity blended with fine sensibility. Those who have got from Johnson the idea that Donne was a clever but chilly trifler should study his correspondence. I quote one passage, written probably a few years after his marriage, when he was in despair over the uncertainty of his fortunes and the unprofitableness of his life:

'Every Tuesday I make account that I turn a great hour-glass and consider that a week's life is run out since I writ. But if I ask myself what I have done in the last watch or would do in the next, I can say nothing; if I say that I have passed it without hurting any, so may the spider in my window. The primitive monks were excusable in their retirings and enclosures of themselves; for even of them every one cultivated his own garden and orchard, that is, his soul and body, by meditation and manufactures; and they sought the world no more since they consumed none of her sweetness, nor begot others to burden her. But for me, if I were able to husband all my time so thriftily as not only not to wound my soul in a minute by actual sin, but not to rob and cozen her by giving any part to pleasure or business, but to bestow it all upon her in meditation, yet even in that I should wound her more and contract another guiltiness; as the eagle were very unnatural, if, because she is able to do it, she should perch a whole day upon a tree, staring in contemplation of the majesty and glory of the sun, and let her young eaglets starve in the nest.'

From the time Donne entered the Church — he was then forty-two years old — there was not a moment's doubt about his reputation or his future prospects. He advanced from preferment to preferment, and at last reached the high position of Dean of Saint Paul's, which he filled till his death. That he was happy would be too much to say. His Christian faith was never shaken, but the feverish restlessness of his nature and his constant brooding on the sins of the past cut him off from any settled peace in his religion. In 1617 his wife died. The blow was severe, and he never recovered from it. Even then he was worn and broken in health, and his letters are full, not of complaint, but of reference to the weakness and weariness that hung over him like a cloud. 'I am not alive because I have not had enough to kill me, but because it pleases God to pass me through many infirmities before He takes me, either by those particular remembrances to bring me to a particular repentance, or by them to

give me hope of his particular mercies in heaven.'
Yet he battled on for fourteen years more, indomitable in devotion to the cause he had undertaken
to serve, indomitable in love, indomitable in hope,
though his hope might seem at times a little
shadowy and forlorn.

He performed the duties of his office till the end,
and his last sermon, a solemn discourse on the
solemn text, 'To God the Lord belong the issues of
death,' was delivered when he was so feeble that
many people said he was preaching at his own funeral.

He died on the last day of March, in the year
1631.

Before leaving the biographical part of my subject, I must quote from Walton one striking anecdote:

'Dr. Donne, by the persuasion of Dr. Fox,
easily yielded at this very time to have a monument made for him; but Dr. Fox undertook not to
persuade him how or what monument it should be;
that was left to Dr. Donne himself.

'A monument being resolved upon, Dr. Donne
sent for a carver to make for him in wood the figure
of an urn, giving him directions for the compass and
height of it, and to bring with him a board of the

just height of his body. These being got, then, without delay, a choice painter was got to be in readiness to draw his picture, which was taken as followeth. Several charcoal fires being first made in his large study, he brought with him into that place his winding-sheet in his hand; and having put off all his clothes, had this sheet put on him, and so tied with knots at his head and feet, and his hands so placed as dead bodies are usually fitted to be shrouded, and put into their coffin or grave. Upon this urn he thus stood with his eyes shut with so much of the sheet turned aside as might show his lean, pale, and deathlike face, which was purposely turned toward the east, from whence he expected the second coming of his and our Saviour Jesus. In this posture he was drawn at his just height; and when the picture was fully finished, he caused it to be set by his bedside, where it continued and became his hourly object till his death.'

It would be unjust to Donne to make no mention of his prose writings even in an essay devoted to his poetry. In quantity his prose far exceeds his verse, and the substance of it, though very different from that of his poems, and certainly far less interesting to the general reader, is perhaps quite as much marked by his peculiar qualities of passion and intensity. Sermons form the bulk of Donne's prose work. He has been accused of preaching with the jingle and word-play that are said to injure his poetry. On this point Coleridge remarks: 'I have, and that most carefully, read Dr. Donne's sermons, and find none of these jingles. The great art of the orator, to make whatever he talks of appear of importance — this, indeed, Donne has effected with consummate skill.' Elizabethan sermons are tedious reading; but I do not see how one can go through a sermon of Donne's without agreeing with Coleridge. I can recommend no better specimen for the reader's perusal than the magnificent passage quoted by Mr. A. H. Bullen in his introduction to the works of Marston.

Donne wrote other prose besides sermons, though most of it is religious. One exception, composed in his younger days, is his 'Biathanatos,' an essay in which he attempts to prove that suicide is not in every case unlawful. The book was not published till after his death.

II

I have alluded to Donne's great reputation among his contemporaries. He was in many ways a typical Elizabethan, and his fellows recognized him as such. The reaction 'from this opinion in the eighteenth century was natural. Pope admired Donne's satires; but he considered it necessary to polish and practically rewrite them before presenting them to the delicate palates of his own public. Johnson's opinion I have already referred to. The great censor used Donne as a sort of scapegoat for Cowley, bracketing the two together as representatives of the metaphysical school of poets. This unintelligible epithet was happily chosen to unite two writers who have as little as possible in common. Unfortunately Johnson did not himself define the name. 'The metaphysical poets,' he says, 'were men of learning, and to show their learning was their whole endeavor.' But may not one be learned without being metaphysical? So many men have been metaphysical without being learned! An ingenious defense of this appellation is to be found in Mr. Elwes's 'Life of Pope.' Donne and his fellows, Mr. Elwes argues, and, indeed, the Elizabethans generally, inherited the philosophy of the mediæval schoolmen. From them they got their hair-splitting, wire-drawing subtlety, from them, also, their strange, uncouth conception of the natural world. If this was the case, Johnson was above all things happy in the word he chose. It does not take much to upset this theory, even if there is a grain of truth at the bottom of it. The conclusions Mr. Elwes draws show that there must be a fallacy. The great defect of this metaphysical poetry — so he goes on — was its separation from nature, and to return to nature was the triumph achieved by the school of Pope. Did any one ever before hold up the poetry of Pope as the mirror of nature? The most obscure and elaborate poem of Donne strikes more deeply into the truths of nature and the heart of man than the most brilliant production of the clever rhymer of Twickenham.

If Mr. Elwes had said 'taste' instead of 'nature,' he would have had reason on his side. Good taste, which was the merit of Pope and Addison, was woefully lacking, not only to Donne, but to the Elizabethans generally. It was this want of measure, of a decent reasonableness, which offended Johnson, and made him stand a little on his guard, even against Shakespeare. Good taste, the love of rounded and flawless beauty, Donne did not possess, nor did Cowley; but here the resemblance between them ends. The disregard of perfect clearness and Attic simplicity takes various forms among the different Elizabethan writers. There is

the careless, joyous overflow of imaginative richness, which shows itself, influenced more or less by
foreign pedantry, in the earlier poets, in Sidney's
'Arcadia,' in the novels of Lyly, Lodge, and Greene,
in Shakespeare's plays of the first period. Secondly,
there is the habit of making up for deep, strong
feeling by the use of far-fetched, frigid conceits;
this is more common with the later writers, Cra-
shaw, Habington, Cowley especially; Donne is by
no means wholly free from it. Thirdly, there is a
strangeness, an appearance of labor, resulting from
the intense, crowding energy of the poet's thought,
an energy that cannot stop to arrange its expressions, to choose its figures, that strikes the iron at a
white heat, moulds it, often awkwardly, but always
leaves it with a stamp of power; I cannot propose
a better instance of this than some parts — only
some parts — of Shakespeare and almost the whole
of Donne. Of course, these are all forms of one tendency manifesting itself in different temperaments;
but Donne's was a different temperament from that
of Sidney on the one hand and that of Cowley on
the other. The essence of his poetical gift, the essence of his moral character, was effort, struggle.
No one could be further removed than he from such
simple sweetness as that of Spenser. Donne was

always at war with the elements of style, bending them, rending them, straining them, to match the sweeping tide of his thoughts and passions. Sometimes he conquered, and soared into the highest heaven of poetry; sometimes he was worsted and sank to depths lower than the lowest of prose. The effort he makes in the latter case, the distortions he produces, are painful, like the scratching of a pin on glass, as in the hideous exaggeration so often quoted:

> 'Oh, do not die, for I shall hate
> All women so, when thou art gone,
> That thee I shall not celebrate,
> When I remember thou wast one.'

Alas! it is needless to bring forward further examples.

Another defect of Donne's, more real than his conceits, is his difficulty. Cowley is simple. Conceits are scattered over the natural movement of his writing like red knots on a white garment. Donne is often unintelligible, wantonly so. He flings down his ideas before you like a tangled skein; you meddle with it at your peril. In this, also, he has some affinity with Shakespeare. One can take, almost at random, from Shakespeare's later plays, passages that require very careful reading:

A NATURALIST OF SOULS

'A strange fellow here
Writes me that man, how dearly ever parted,
How much in having, or without, or in,
Cannot make boast to have that which he hath,
Nor feels not what he owes, but by reflection;
As when his virtues shining upon others
Heat them and they retort that heat again
To the first giver.'

Donne, however, writes in this way through whole
poems and with infinitely less art than his great
contemporary, who, when he used such a style, had
his own ends to serve. Donne employed it indif-
ferently on profound philosophical subjects and on
what he meant to be the most rapid and graceful
lyrics. Of the latter I quote a specimen:

'Whilst yet to prove
I thought there was some deity in love,
So did I reverence and gave
Worship as atheists at their dying hour
Call, what they cannot name, an unknown power,
As ignorantly did I crave:
Thus when
Things not yet known are coveted by men,
Our desires give them fashion and so
As they wax lesser, fall, as they size, grow.'

Much of Donne's best writing is contained in his
lyrics, but we must not judge them by the pure and
delicate ease of the exquisite work Mr. Bullen has
given us in his 'Lyrics from Elizabethan Song Books.'

THE POETRY OF DONNE

Still another reason why Donne is little read nowadays is that he is extremely coarse — coarse is the word, rather than sensual, at least for most of his poems. He never shrinks from any expression that throws light on his meaning. No modern realist, no Frenchman, could go further. Shakespeare pales beside him — even Ben Jonson. Literature is full of anomalies: Donne, the coarsest of Elizabethan poets, was the most intensely, profoundly Christian in spirit, the most serious, the most earnest, the highest in his standards and aims. Oh, irony of genius!

III

Donne is always regarded as an example of rough and jarring metre. Dr. Johnson said of the 'metaphysical poets' that 'instead of writing poetry they only wrote verses, and very often such verses as stood the test of the finger better than that of the ear'; while the earlier and greater Jonson told Drummond 'that Donne, for not keeping of accent, deserved hanging.' It would be foolish to deny the extreme, absurd harshness of many of Donne's lines. The defect is so evident that it seems as if Donne himself must have been well aware of it, especially as he often shows an exquisite sense of rhythm. This is no excuse. It does, however, suggest that he had an artistic aim in the very halt of his verses. The conclusion is strengthened when we find that his satires are rougher than his lyrics and serious pieces. As might be expected with so difficult a writer, the text of early editions is extremely corrupt, which accounts for some of his metrical irregularities.

Yet nothing can palliate Donne's wanton disregard of the laws of English versification. Coleridge said: 'Read even Donne's satires as he meant them to be read, and as the sense and passion demand, and you will find in the lines a manly harmony.' This may be true of the continuous effect in long passages; but it is not true of single lines.

'A subtle statesman may gather of that.'

'His passions and the world's troubles; rock me.'

Words are split to make a rhyme, accents are shaken over the verse from a pepper-box, the reader thinks himself adrift in chaos. Yet it would be simplicity to confound Donne's rhythm with that of an incompetent poetaster. He is never commonplace, never monotonous, never tame. Beneath his apparent carelessness there is profound skill in the variation of pauses, in the management of periods. Mr.

THE POETRY OF DONNE

Swinburne has well said the verse of Donne is rugged, the verse of Jonson stiff, meaning just this, that Donne's roughness is mainly intentional and calculated to contribute to the force and effect of the idea conveyed.

In truth, when the merits of Donne's versification are considered, he will be a bold man that will venture to make excuses for him. I do not know that any English poet has surpassed the vigor of movement in even the harshest of his satires, though they are difficult to quote.

> 'Sir, though (I thank God for it) I do hate
> All this town perfectly, yet there's one state
> In all ill things so excellently best
> That hate towards that breeds pity towards the rest.'

>   'Words, words, which would tear
> The tender labyrinth of a maid's soft ear
> More, more than ten Slavonians' scoldings, more
> Than when winds in our ruined abbeys roar.'

And in Donne's poems, everywhere, there are lines of extraordinary rhythmic power, like the following from one of his 'Holy Sonnets':

> 'At the round earth's imagined corners blow
> Your trumpets, Angels, and arise, arise
> From death you numberless infinities
> Of souls and to your scattered bodies go.'

But Donne's verse has beauty and sweetness as

well as force. He can tune it at times, in short passages, to an exquisite subtlety of delicate music:

> 'So may thy mighty, amazing beauty move
> Envy in all women and in all men love.'

Take also the following lines from 'The Calm'; the harshness of sound and sense in the first two contrasts strikingly with the grace and melancholy cadence of the last:

> 'As water did in storms, now pitch runs out
> As lead when a fired church becomes one spout, —
> And all our beauty and our trim decays,
> Like court removing or like ended plays.'[1]

Donne's lyrics, especially, are full of evidence that his fault in verse-writing was carelessness, not lack of ear. Take such little turns as this:

> 'If thou find'st one, let me know;
> Such a pilgrimage were sweet,'

or the whole song of which the following is the first stanza:

> 'Sweetest Love, I do not go
> For weariness of thee,
> Nor in hope the world can show
> A fitter love for me;

---

[1] Curiously enough, the last line occurs, with slight variations in Jonson's *New Inn* (IV. 3). This play must have been written long after Donne's poem, so that he could not have been the borrower. Jonson greatly admired 'The Calm.'

But since that I
Must die at last, 'tis best
Thus to use myself in jest,
By feigned deaths to die.'

Yet it must be admitted that Donne's peculiar excellence is not metrical. The ruggedness, the force that stamps his verse is far more characteristic of his thought. He ransacks all nature for an image that will not dull the intensity of his feelings, and he thus falls into the vagaries that horrified Dr. Johnson. But the originality and startling effectiveness of his figures have never been surpassed. He darts a flash of lightning on his object, strips it of all conventional trapping, with a grasp recalling Dante in power, if not in simplicity. Here is a most Dantesque and terrible simile from the 'Second Anniversary':

'As sometimes in a beheaded man,
Though at those two red seas which freely ran
One from the trunk, another from the head,
His soul has sailed to her eternal bed,
His eyes will twinkle and his tongue will roll,
As though he beckoned and called back his soul,
He grasps his hands and he pulls up his feet,
And seems to reach and to step forth to meet
His soul; when all these motions which we saw
Are but as ice that crackles at a thaw;
Or as a lute, which in moist weather, rings
Her knell alone by cracking of her strings;

> So struggles this dead world now she is gone:
> For there is motion in corruption.'

Beside which place the following, with its subtle and melancholy charm:

> 'But when old age their beauty hath in chase
> And ploughs up furrows in their once smooth face,
> Then they become forsaken and do show
> Like stately abbeys ruined long ago.'

Let me in passing point out that in both these passages the rhythm is striking as well as the thought.

Donne's originality and power show not only in elaborate figures, but in little touches constantly occurring. In 'The Anagram':

> 'If we might put the letters but one way
> In that *lean dearth* of words what could we say?'

In the 'Second Anniversary':

> 'Shalt thou not find a *spungy, slack* divine
> Drink and suck in the instructions of great men
> And for the word of God vent them again?'

From a letter to the Lady Cary:

> 'For when, through tasteless, flat humility,
> In *dough-baked* men some harmlessness we see,
> 'Tis but his phlegm that's virtuous and not he.'

The same qualities, vigor, and intensity rather than tenderness or grace, mark Donne's description of nature. He did, indeed, write of

> 'The household bird with the red stomacher,'

and with Shakespearean sweetness of

> 'Lilies, hyacinths, and your gorgeous birth
> Of all pied flowers which diaper the earth';

but he draws generally with a pen of iron, and his landscape has a taste of Salvator. The companion pieces called 'The Storm' and 'The Calm' are good instances. In the latter, a most remarkable poem, it is interesting to compare his

> 'And in one place lay
> Feathers and dust to-day and yesterday,'

with Keats's

> 'Not so much life as on a summer's day
> Lifts not one light seed from the feathered grass,
> But where the dead leaf fell there did it rest.'

The traits we have hitherto studied in Donne must make it evident that he would succeed in satire, and his writing in that kind is, indeed, masterly. It is not necessary to settle whether he was the first of English satirists in date: for quality, no other can be placed beside him in his own line. His subjects do not require the broad canvases of Dryden, nor has he Dryden's lucidity and rapidity. But even Dryden cannot approach him in power, and he makes Pope seem dry and tame. Of his own contemporaries Hall is far more conventional,

Wither thinner, though certainly clearer. Marston has a touch of Donne's force, but is more grotesque and labored. His satires are difficult from affectation. Donne's, like all his work, are moulded directly and naturally by the stern and tumultuous cast of his thought. He ploughs his way along, regardless of obstacles, tearing up language and metre by the roots; but his result is unequaled. Obscurity and coarseness will keep his satires from ever becoming popular, but no one has studied them carefully without being repaid. How the characters stand out! With what energy he lashes the vices and follies around him! Here is his account of an interview with a court bore:

> 'I tell him of new plays:
> He takes my hand and as a still which stays
> A semibrief 'twixt each drop, he niggardly,
> As loath to enrich me, so tells many a lie
> More than ten Hollinsheds, or Halls or Stows,
> Of trivial household trash he knows: he knows
> When the queen frowned or smiled; and he knows what
> A subtle statesman may gather of that.
> He knows who loves whom; and who by poison
> Hastes to an office's reversion.
> He knows who hath sold his land and now doth beg
> A license old iron, boots, shoes, and egg-
> Shells to transport. . . .
>   And wiser than all us,
> He knows what lady is not painted.'

All this is lightened and enlivened by keen wit. He comments thus on a young man of fashion:

> 'His schools
> Are ordinaries where civil men seem fools;
> Or are for being there; his best books, plays,
> Where meeting godly scenes, perhaps he prays.
> His first set prayer was for his father ill
> And sick — that he might die; that had, until
> The lands were gone, he troubled God no more.'

And here is a scrap of one of his dialogues:

> 'Now leaps he upright, jogs me, and cries, "Do you see
> Yonder well-favoured youth?" "Which?" "Oh! 'Tis he
> That dances so divinely." "Oh!" said I,
> "Stand still, must you dance too for company?"
> He drooped.'

This admirable comic gift is shown not only in Donne's satires, but in almost all his poems, and atones for many of his extravagances. Often, if you look carefully, you can see a half smile on his face that you should take him seriously. The richness and variety of his humor appear in such poems as 'Woman's Constancy,' 'The Triple Fool' with its

> 'Who are a little wise the best fools be,'

'Love's Legacy,' and in flashes everywhere. Something in this mingling of mirth with passion, this swift interchange of grief and laughter, recalls Heine; but Donne had nothing of the cynic about him. The thing above all others that makes him beautiful and lovable is his tenderness, which separates him absolutely from the mockery of Heine, and still more from the savage invective of satirists like Marston, with whom I but now compared him.

IV

As a poet and as a man Donne does, indeed, rise far above mere railers at humanity and life. His smile is that of sympathy, not that of scorn. His philosophy was too deep, his nature too serious, to allow him ever to be a trifler, jester, scoffer. His high intellectual earnestness never leaves him even in matters that seem light and trifling. He never shuns the struggle with great problems. One does not go to poets or to Elizabethans for consistent philosophical reasoning; but in acute, thoughtful, and far-reaching comment on human life Donne is unsurpassed. Instances of this are best taken from his 'Verse-Letters,' where the dignity of tone is least often marred by conceit and strangeness. Here is one from a letter to Sir Henry Wotton:

'Be thou thine own home and in thyself dwell;
Inn anywhere, continuance maketh Hell.
And seeing the snail, which everywhere doth roam,

> Carrying his own house still, is still at home,
> Follow (for he is easy-paced) this snail,
> Be thy own palace, or the world's thy jail.'

And another, to the same effect:

> 'Seek we then ourselves in ourselves; for as
> Men force the sun with much more force to pass
> By gathering his beams with a crystal glass,
>
> 'So we, if we into ourselves will turn,
> Blowing our sparks of virtue, may outburn
> The straw which doth about our hearts sojourn.'

Above all, there is the noble letter to Sir Henry Goodyere. The following introductory stanza is not above the rest:

> 'Who makes the last a pattern for next year
> Turns no new leaf but still the same things reads,
> Seen things he sees, heard things again doth hear,
> And makes his life but like a pair of beads.'

Intellect, thought, is certainly predominant in Donne. It was predominant in all the Elizabethan poets. All of them, unless we except Spenser, were ready to wander off in endless deserts of ingenious speculation. The very titles of their poems → 'A Treatise of Monarchy,' 'Musophilus,' 'The Immortality of the Soul,' 'The Anatomy of the Soul' — show a taste for abstraction, not to say pedantry. But intellectual as they are, they all have imagination, passion. Compare Donne with Emerson and this point becomes clear. Emerson has no greater fancy for epigram, for cleverness, than the older poet, but he is always cold, never touched, fired, carried away. Donne at his strangest is stung with intense feeling; he blends beauty and grace with his harshest rhythms, with the subtlest refinements of his thought. This is his supreme excellence, the merit that makes one overlook all his faults, if it does not outweigh them. This lifts him a whole heaven above the ease of Waller and the sweetness of Cowley. He is real, he is alive. In satire, in elegy, in love lyric, in hymn, his words burn, and the reader who feels cannot but be kindled by them.

This intensity is not found in all Donne's poems alike. It is not, I think, found so perfectly in the two celebrated 'Anniversaries,' written in memory of Elizabeth Drury, as in some others shorter and less known. The first 'Anniversary,' especially, does not give the most favorable view of Donne's singular genius. It was composed to eulogize a lady Donne had never known; it is consequently general and full of expressions that are exceedingly repulsive. The second is much better, in parts giving Donne at his best, as in the wonderful lines:

> 'Her pure and eloquent blood
> Spoke in her cheeks and so distinctly wrought
> That one might almost say her body thought.'

Still, even in this great poem there is a good deal that is difficult and affected.

The same faults mar Donne's only attempt at narrative, the fragmentary 'Progress of the Soul.'

The 'Elegies' and, above all, the 'Lyrics,' are Donne's most satisfactory productions. The elegies are, unfortunately, difficult to quote, though who could pass by the charming 'Refusal to Allow His Young Wife to Accompany Him Abroad,' or the 'Autumnal,' or the one 'Upon the Loss of His Mistress' Chain,' with its keen wit and its Shakespearean line:

> 'So lean, so pale, so lame, so ruinous'?

But I confess, of all Donne's works his lyrics are to me the most delightful in their wisdom, their humor, their passion, their varying play of sense and sound. Has any one ever flashed the light of imagination so vividly upon the depths of feeling? Now he does this by a simple, almost careless touch, as in that line of the 'Relic' so much praised by Lowell, which describes the openers of the poet's grave as finding

> 'A bracelet of bright hair about the bone' —

just that one word 'bright' gleams like a star; or as in 'Love's Legacy':

> 'And all your graces no more use will have
> Than a sun-dial in a grave.'

Now he twists a wreath of faint, sweet, strange thoughts about a subject almost grotesque, which yet under his hands becomes intensely real, as in 'Air and Angels':

> 'Ever thy hair for love to work upon
> Is much too much, some fitter must be sought,
> For nor in nothing, nor in things
> Extreme and scattering bright came love in here;
> Then as an angel face and wings
> Of air not pure as it, yet pure doth wear,
> So thy love may be my lover's sphere;
> Just such disparity
> As is 'twixt air and angels' purity,
> 'Twixt woman's love and man's will ever be.'

Now he inserts in a poem made up of curious subtleties a few lines of the most solemn and touching dignity, like the conclusion of the lyrical 'Anniversary':

> 'Let us live nobly, and live, and live again
> Years and years unto years, till we attain
> To write threescore: this is the second of our reign.'

In his lyrics the necessity of passion often saves Donne from using conceits, makes the conceits tolerable or even impressive when they come. This is illustrated by the whole poem called 'A Valediction of Tears,' also by the one 'Upon Parting from His Mistress,' which contains in a stanza condemned by Johnson, but praised by most critics, the comparison of himself and her to a pair of compasses:

'Thy soul, the fixed foot, makes no show
To move, but doth if the other do.

And though it in the centre sit,
Yet when the other far doth roam,
It leans and hearkens after it,
And grows erect as that comes home.'

One thing that must be noticeable even in what I have already quoted from Donne is the prominence through all his poetry of death and the grave. An uneasy curiosity about these matters is a trait of the Renaissance. Epicureans like Herrick constantly refer to them, sometimes from a sort of fascination, sometimes merely to enhance the zest of present pleasure. But with Donne it is far different. He was no Epicurean, no Pagan; he was only in part a child of the Renaissance. His wildest verse bears the mark of those laborious years spent in comparing the doctrines of the Catholic and Protestant churches. His entrance into the ministry was no abrupt change or conversion. One is sure that he never plunged carelessly into mad riot, as did Marlowe and Greene. If he tried violent pleasures, it was uneasily, reluctantly, half in bravado, despair at the uncertainty and vanity of anything else. No other English poet has ever been so penetrated with the restlessness, the wretchedness of life as Donne. In his 'Devotions' he says, 'Man hath no centre but misery.' In his letters he appears always occupied with death, almost in love with it. The same feeling is shown in that curious anecdote about his monument. One finds it again and again in his most passionate poems:

> 'I hate extremes; yet I had rather stay
> With graves than cradles to wear out a day.'

See, above all, the strange and somber lyric entitled 'A Nocturnal on Saint Lucy's Day.'

No Schopenhauer or Leopardi could more urge the imperfection of our earthly life than Donne, but the difference is that Donne was a Christian. I should, perhaps, make some allusion here to Donne's especially religious poetry. It has the same energy and passion as his other work. Take, for example, the striking 'Hymn to Christ on the Author's Last Going into Germany,' of which I quote the first stanza with its movement swift and overwhelming as the mystical devotion it illustrates:

'In what torn ship soever I embark,
  That ship shall be my emblem of thy ark;
  What sea soever swallow me, that flood
  Shall be to me an emblem of thy blood.
  Though thou with clouds of anger do disguise
  Thy face, yet through that mask I know those eyes,
  Which though they turn away sometimes, they never will
      despise.'

But the intensity and profound earnestness of Christian thought belong to Donne's secular poems also. This separates him not only from modern pessimists, but from his literary contemporaries, from the serene naturalism of Shakespeare, from the stern stoicism of Milton and Marvell. At any rate, his Christianity was of a different type from theirs. To him the essence of our life here was struggle and war. He never lost sight of the goal, the star of faith was never overclouded for him; but the flesh was unequal to the spirit. He loved no eremitical solitude. He moved amid the bustle and confusion of cities and courts. He knew all temptations and was led astray by them. But he always hated them, he never yielded, never despaired. Through sin and wretchedness he fought his way upward, and the stamp of strife is left on all he ever wrote, not only on his sermons, but on the freest of his verses; all alike are the passionate expression of one of the noblest, tenderest, broadest, and deepest natures that ever received the subtle gift of genius. It is for this that Donne must remain preëminently great to those who will labor with him; not for his wit, nor his learning, nor his eccentricity. He has not the ingenious sanctity of Herbert, nor the lark-like loveliness and bright simplicity of Vaughan, nor the serene elevation of Giles Fletcher; but he has the moral dignity and grandeur of a soul which, not ignorant of the wretchedness of this world, is yet forever ravished with the love and worship of the eternal.

1892

IV
A PESSIMIST POET

IV

A PESSIMIST POET

I

GIACOMO LEOPARDI was born on the 29th of June, 1798, at Recanati, a small town in the March of Ancona. His father, Count Monaldo, was of an old family, but not wealthy. He was a scholar and an author, but full of aristocratic prejudice, and opposed to reform, either political or religious. His wife seems not to have had much influence over her children; at least, they write to her and of her with respect, but with little affection.

Giacomo was the eldest of the family. Brought up in the solitude of a provincial Italian city, he buried himself in books, which alone offered him access to the world. The account of his youthful studies is prodigious. When fifteen years old he set himself to learn Greek without a teacher, and succeeded so well that in the following year he was able to write a commentary on Porphyrius's 'Life of Plotinus.' He also made himself familiar with Hebrew and the modern languages, except German.

These studies soon gained him a name. One of the first results of them was a friendship with Pietro

Giordani, which lasted during Leopardi's life. His letters to Giordani form a large portion of his correspondence; and they give us a good idea of his early years — of the various difficulties he had to contend with in his literary pursuits, and of the formation of that peculiar philosophy which is always associated with his name. In the first place, his enthusiastic study had broken his health. 'I often endure for many hours,' he writes, 'the horrible torment of sitting with my hands folded.' And again: 'Ah, my dear Giordani, what do you think I do nowadays? Get up in the morning late, because now — a diabolical state of things — I prefer sleeping to waking. Then get immediately to walking and walk without ever opening my mouth or seeing a book till dinner. After dinner walk likewise till supper; unless by making a great effort, often stopping and sometimes giving up altogether, I manage to read for an hour.'

Ill-health was not the only cause of Leopardi's melancholy. He found himself condemned to pass the best years of his life in a small provincial town. He was not naturally inclined to see good in everything — rather, he spoiled every possibility of present pleasure by dwelling on an imaginary future; and his abuse of his native place is extremely violent. 'What is there beautiful in Recanati? What is there that a man would take pains to see or learn? Nothing. Now, God has made this world of ours so beautiful, men have made so many beautiful things in it, there are so many men in it, that any one in his senses burns to see and know. The earth is full of wonders, and I, at eighteen, must say, "In this den shall I live and die where I was born?" Do you think these desires can be bridled, that they are un-just, tyrannous, extravagant, that it is folly to be dissatisfied with seeing nothing, to be discontented with Recanati?' In this passage we see Leopardi's weakness: he was always talking about love, he was gentle and affectionate to his friends; yet he was haughty, too forgetful of sympathy and human kindness. In the same way he talked about philoso-phy and studied it; but he never possessed that su-preme philosophy of life which teaches us to take the world as we find it and respect facts.

There was yet another source of the unhappiness of our poet. If the boy — for at this time he was hardly more — had found comfort at home, Reca-nati might have seemed tolerable. But his mother was nothing to him; Count Monaldo approved his son's taste for philology, but they differed on phi-losophy and on politics. Their relations were altogether unfortunate, owing to misunderstandings and to general incompatibility. Biographers at first sided with Giacomo. Of late years some things have come up to excuse the old Count; yet the following sketch of him, taken from his own autobiography, will show what his character was: 'The experience of my whole life has taught me the truth of the saying — Seneca's, I believe — that there is no great intelligence without its dose of madness, and I have been surprised to see that in some corner of the loftiest mind there lurk incredible puerilities. I have made some examination of myself in order to learn the weak point of my reason, and not having found any, I am tempted to believe my mind superior to many, not indeed in loftiness, but in balance.' Poverty obliged Monaldo to deny his son many things, and Giacomo was but too ready to assume a harsher motive.

A close affection bound the young scholar to his brother Carlo and to his sister Paolina, who seem, nevertheless, to have been greatly his inferiors. One person only in his family might have been really helpful to him — his aunt, Ferdinanda Melchiorri, who, unfortunately, died when he was twenty-four years old. The few letters of hers which Signor Piergili has collected show a mind of great clearness, a sensibility equal to Leopardi's, and a calmness and resignation he was never able to attain. 'Little by little we learn to forget our miseries by slighting them or by not keeping the image of them forever before us; reason must persuade us of this, and we must use reason for our happiness, not for the contrary.' You see Leopardi lost much when he lost her.

The life at Recanati — living death he would have called it — with its tedium, its fierce protest against the tyranny of circumstances, its idealization of the outside world, continued till the man's nature was thoroughly confirmed in a philosophy of defiance. The influence of Giordani had separated him from the Catholic Church, and filled him with liberal ideas; yet he never adopted these ideas with great enthusiasm — they were sweet illusions, but illusions.

In 1822 he finally succeeded in getting away and going to Rome. It is pitiful, even if a little amusing, to see his disappointment. Rome is no better than Recanati, after all. 'Speaking seriously,' he writes to his sister, 'you may take it as certain that the most stolid Recanatese has a greater dose of good sense than the wisest and gravest Roman. Believe me, when I say that the frivolity of these idiots is beyond anything. If I tried to narrate all the absurd stuff which serves as matter for their talk, and which they revel in, a folio would not suffice.' Truly, *cœlum mutat, non animum.*

Leopardi went to Rome to get recognition and encouragement in his studies, and also to seek some sort of employment that would enable him to live away from the detested Recanati. Reputation as a scholar soon came to him, though such work as his was better appreciated by foreigners than by his fellow countrymen. Bunsen, then Prussian ambassador at Rome, treated him kindly, and Niebuhr expressed great admiration for him. We read in 'A Memoir of Baron Bunsen' that Niebuhr, 'returning from his visit to the wretched lodging of Leopardi, entered the office-room at Palazzo Savelli, where Bunsen was at work, exclaiming, with an unwonted burst of satisfaction, that he had at last seen an Italian worthy of the old Italians and of the ancient Romans.' But admiration came more readily than preferment. The ecclesiastical authorities at Rome were willing to do what they could, but only on condition that Leopardi should enter the Church. In order to bring this about, they deferred giving him even an insignificant lay office, hoping literally to starve him into obedience to their wishes. But his so-called 'philosophical conversion' had taken hold of him too deeply for honest acquiescence in Catholic doctrine; and the inflexible uprightness which marked him, as it has some other unbelievers, made him scorn a hypocritical compliance. Therefore, after lingering on at Rome through the winter, he was obliged to return to his father's house.

Recanati did not seem any more agreeable than formerly. His ill-health continued to make study impossible, and he was driven back upon his own thoughts; which fill his letters at this time — chiefly to Giordani and to Brighenti, a Bolognese friend — with an endless monotony of wretchedness. In the year 1824 he published at Bologna a collection of poems, most of which were new. He also published the first of his philosophical prose works — 'A comparison of the Opinions of the Younger Brutus and of Theophrastus, on the Approach of Death.'

In the spring of 1825 he once more left Recanati — this time intending to proceed by way of Bologna to Milan, where he had engaged to do various kinds of literary work for the publisher Stella. He found Bologna very attractive. His reputation had preceded him thither, and the literary circle received him cordially. In Milan it was different. He had no friends, no connections. Stella's work was disagreeable to him — editing, with little or no prospect of either freedom or great profit. After a stay of two months, he returned to Bologna, having arranged to carry out his agreement with Stella at that place.

The next year was perhaps the happiest, or the least miserable, of his life. His health was, as always, bad; he had little money, and was obliged to give lessons, like many another unfortunate man of letters. But he was in the company of people who made much of him, and he found the social diversion that was lacking in Recanati. 'These lessons,' he writes to his brother Carlo, 'which eat out the heart of my day, bore me horribly. Except for that, I have nothing to complain of. The literary men, who in the beginning, as I have been told, looked upon me with envy and mistrust, expecting to find me haughty and disposed to put on airs, are now well pleased with my affability and readiness to give way to every one; in short, they speak very well of me, and I feel that they consider my presence an acquisition to Bologna.' At this time, also, we find the trace of one of his few love affairs — that with the Countess Malvezzi. The bodily weakness, amounting almost to deformity, which resulted from his early studies, made him painfully sensitive in his relations with women; but in this particular case literary sympathy seems to have been added to merely social attractions. 'When I first knew her,' he writes, 'I lived in a sort of delirium and fever. We have never spoken of love, unless in jest, but we keep up a tender and sympathetic friendship, with mutual interest, and a freedom that is like love without love's disquietude.' Alas, such 'sympathetic friendships' hasten so quickly to their end!

In the autumn of 1826, Leopardi returned to Recanati. From this time on his life was a losing struggle with ill-health. His hatred of his native place grew more and more bitter: 'It seems a thousand years till I can escape from this hoggish city, where I know not whether the men are more fools or knaves; I know well that they are both one and the other.' Harsh notes like this occur too often in Leopardi; yet his situation was undoubtedly a trying one.

In 1827–28, we find him at Pisa, the climate there suiting him better than at Florence or Bologna. The death of his younger brother Luigi at this time called forth a few words which it is well to quote, in contrast with the passage just given: 'I have lost a brother in the flower of his years: my family in their grief looks for no other consolation than that of my return. I should be ashamed to live, if anything but a perfect and utter impossibility prevented me from going to shed my tears with those I love.'

He did, indeed, return to Recanati for another winter; but in May, 1830, he left there for the last time. For the next three years he lived in Florence and Rome, his health getting steadily worse and worse. Finally, in the autumn of 1833, he went to Naples with Antonio Ranieri, whose name is inseparably connected with Leopardi's later years. After this the letters gathered in the correspondence become few and brief, being chiefly pitiful requests for money to make him less dependent on his friends. Extreme weakness rendered any continuous work impossible; and it was probably only the constant and affectionate care of Ranieri and his sister that prolonged the poet's life. They were successful in doing this till the spring of 1837. Then, quite suddenly, death came on the 14th of June, caused by dropsy affecting the heart. The cholera was in the city at the time, and Ranieri was only able to secure private burial for his friend by bribing the priest of the little church of San Vitale with a present of fish.

A PESSIMIST POET

Leopardi's prose is either philological or philosophical. The philological work belongs chiefly to
his younger days. It is now, of course, much out of
date; Leopardi had no idea of the discoveries that
have been made in the nineteenth century as to the
relationship of the different European languages.
Yet he was undoubtedly a thorough scholar, and
probably had that delicate insight which goes so
much farther than erudition, and which so many
great scholars have been without. Perhaps his
most permanent effort of this kind is his translation
of various classical authors, executed with the care
and patient search for accurate expression that
mark all his work. The excellence of his scholarship
appears in his imitations of Greek and old Italian
writers, which long deceived some very learned
men. The chief original product of his early years
was a book on the 'Popular Errors of the Ancients,'
written when he was seventeen years old, and showing certainly extraordinary learning for a boy of that
age. Outside of the curious citations, the reader
will find little to interest him here — nothing of
the large Renaissance curiosity that informs the
fascinating work of Sir Thomas Browne. In treat-
ing the superstitions of Greece and Rome, Leopardi

manifests the same dogmatic spirit that appears in his later writings; only he had not yet hit upon extreme pessimism, nor even left the fold of the Catholic Church. The book closes with this apostrophe: 'Religion, loveliest of things, it is indeed sweet to be able to end with speech of thee that which has been undertaken to do some good to those whom every day thou benefitest; it is indeed sweet to conclude in security and confidence of heart that he is no philosopher who does not follow and respect thee, nor is there any one who follows and respects thee who is not a philosopher.' We are in the full vein of the 'Imitation.'

In a few years the tone changes. Acquaintance with Giordani and others brought about the 'philosophical conversion'; and after that Leopardi's letters are full of attacks upon the system of nature which creates man for useless, purposeless misery. All his remaining prose works not strictly philological develop these views in one form or another. The list is not extensive — some two dozen dialogues and about a hundred 'Thoughts' varying from two to thirty or forty lines. Any one who goes to these writings expecting to find in them the formal and logical exposition of the great German metaphysicians will be disappointed. Leopardi was anxious to teach what he considered to be the true doctrines of philosophy; but his first instinct as an author was literary. The model he had before him was Plato, or, still more, Lucian; and he aimed to convey his teaching by illustration, even allegory, rather than by a system of laborious deduction. Whatever may be thought of his conclusions, his methods have the great merit of simplicity and literary charm.

As to the matter of his philosophy, the general character of it is well known; it consists in an ever-renewed proclamation that the sole certainty of man's life is misery, that the universe exists for no apparent purpose, that if there are gods at all, they only augment the wretchedness of man; though on this last point Leopardi is always reticent, leaving it to the reader to infer the complete incompatibility of any divine love or goodness with such a system as he insists on finding out in nature. It is not necessary to look far for passages illustrating these things. Here is one from a letter written when he was twenty-one years old: 'This is the wretched condition of humanity and the barbarous teaching of reason, that, human joys and griefs being mere illusions, work that is based on the certainty of the nothingness of things is the only work that is just and true. And if it be argued that by regulating all our lives on the feeling of this nothingness, we should end the world and should justly be called mad, it is nevertheless logically certain that this would be madness rational in every respect and even that compared with it all wisdom would be madness; since this world goes on only by the simple and continual forgetfulness of this universal truth that everything is nothing.'

This instantly recalls an eloquent passage from a more celebrated philosopher than Leopardi: 'Rather do we freely acknowledge that what remains after the entire abolition of Will is for all those who are still full of Will certainly nothing; but, conversely, to those in whom the Will has turned and has denied itself, this our world, with all its suns and milky ways, is nothing.' Indeed, the names of Schopenhauer and Leopardi are often associated together more closely than is justified by the circumstances of the case. Schopenhauer's philosophy consists of two parts, which, though skillfully and intimately blended, may yet be separated, and have not, I venture to think, so vital a connection as is generally assumed. The metaphysical part is the theory of Will as Thing-in-Itself constituting the absolute basis of the floating world of phenomena, manifesting itself momentarily in consciousness, then dissolving and vanishing again into the unknown from whence it came. The practical part is the unwearied assertion of the utter misery of man's mortal life — misery alleviated only by the encouragement of false and foolish illusions, which make him believe he is ever approaching nearer to what it is impossible he should attain. Whether Schopenhauer deduced his practical doctrine from his abstract theory, or whether, as seems more probable, his empirical view at least colored his metaphysics, I cannot say; at any rate, the two components fit together very neatly.

Of these two elements of Schopenhauer's 'World as Will and Idea,' only one appears in Leopardi. Schopenhauer found him a most satisfactory exponent of his doctrine as to the evil of existence. 'No one,' he says, 'has so thoroughly and exhaustively handled this subject as in our own day Leopardi. He is entirely filled and penetrated by it; his theme is everywhere the mockery and wretchedness of this life; he presents it upon every page of his works, yet in such a multiplicity of forms and applications, with such a wealth of imagery, that he never wearies us, but, on the contrary, is throughout entertaining and exciting.' Indeed, the Italian poet's proclamation of pessimism is so thorough and consistent that it could not but be gratifying to his German follower. Of metaphysics proper, however, Leopardi has little or nothing. He has a great deal to say about philosophy, and about the importance of giving it a place in Italian literature; but in his works he never does more than reiterate a few phrases about the misery of life and the inanity of all human pursuits. Such theory as he has would seem to be derived from the English empirical school of Locke and his followers. He was not a German scholar, and evidently knew nothing even of Kant, much less of Kant's successors. Except for a few coincidences of expression, he has no trace of the elaborate system of Schopenhauer, and would probably have found talk about the Will as Thing-in-Itself simply unintelligible.

Nevertheless, Schopenhauer is right in saying that Leopardi presents the mockery and wretchedness of this life upon every page of his works, and with a multiplicity of forms and illustrations. I think the philosopher is mistaken when he declares that this is always entertaining and exciting; but it is done with such skill that, considering the narrowness of the subject, there is wonderfully little monotony. Every dialogue ends with the same refrain: it were better not to have been born; having been born, it is best to die as soon as convenient; but this theme is constantly varied. Sometimes, as in the 'Hercules and Atlas,' or 'The Earth and the Moon,' superhuman beings satirize the unhappy lot of mortals. Sometimes philosophers discuss it, as in the 'Dialogue between a Physicist and a Metaphysician,' or in the 'Plotinus and Porphyrius.' Sometimes a forlorn creature addresses a higher power with reproach or prayer, as in the 'Dialogue between Nature and a Soul,' or in that 'Between Nature and an Icelander.' Sometimes the misery of man receives illustration or comment from beings lower in the natural world, as in the 'Dialogue between a Will-o'-the-Wisp and a Gnome,' or in the 'Eulogy of Birds.'

The very titles show how much there is of literary art in all these. Some of them are playful — at least on the surface. Hercules persuades Atlas to use the earth for a game of ball, in the midst of which they drop it, greatly to their dismay. Fashion points out to Death the immense services she renders her by leading mankind into infinite pernicious follies. A passer-by questions an almanac-vender as to the coming year, and tries to prove to him that

there is no reason why that should be happy, if
none of the past have been. Some are poetical, almost lyrical, like the 'Song of the Wild Cock,' and
the exquisite 'Eulogy of Birds.' The latter, especially, is an Aristophanic piece of musical grace.
'Other animals appear commonly grave and solemn. . . ; if they take pleasure in the green fields, in
broad and pleasant prospects, in splendid sunshine,
in a crystalline and gentle air, they make no sign.
. . . But birds show their joy by their movements
and their very look.'

Most of the dialogues are, however, of a gray
and melancholy cast. The 'History of the Human
Race,' the first in the collection, gives anything
but a cheerful account of the gradual degradation
of humanity down to the nineteenth century, which
Leopardi detested with all his soul. The 'Wager
of Prometheus' recounts Prometheus's efforts to
prove the excellence of his invention of man, and
his complete failure to do so. 'Copernicus' ridicules
the fluctuations of science. The 'Dialogue between
Frederick Ruysch and his Mummies' represents
the latter as reviving for a short space and enlight-
ening their owner about the other world, as well as
about the departure from this.

Perhaps as complete an exposition as any of

A PESSIMIST POET

Leopardi's pessimism is to be found in the 'Dialogue between Nature and an Icelander.' The native of the northern island, after seeking everywhere the author of the miseries of life, finds in the center of Africa a vast image of a woman, who condescends to discuss the matter with him. She points out that the universe exists only by a continual process of production and destruction. 'That is what all the philosophers argue,' says the Icelander, 'but inasmuch as that which is destroyed suffers, and that which destroys receives no pleasure and is soon destroyed in its turn, tell me what no philosopher can tell me: who is pleased or benefited by this most miserable existence of the universe, sustained by the suffering and death of all things that compose it?' The interesting response to this question is interrupted by the arrival of two hungry lions, who proceed at once to make away with the curious Icelander.

The 'Memorable Sayings of Filippo Ottonieri' gives a sort of idealized sketch of Leopardi himself, embodying the curious combination of defiant nihilism with high moral principle which was peculiar to him. The piece ends with an epitaph of singular and melancholy dignity. 'The bones of Filippo Ottonieri, born for virtuous deeds and for glory, lived indolent and useless, and died without fame, not ignorant of his own nature nor of his own fortune.'

Besides the 'Dialogues' or 'Operette Morali' Leopardi wrote, shortly before his death, about a hundred 'Thoughts,' much the same in tone as his longer pieces. They are, however, colder and more gloomy. Now and then there is a touch of calm insight, as: 'There is no greater mark of feeble philosophy and little wisdom than to demand that the whole of life should be philosophical and wise.' But the majority are quite as cynical as La Rochefoucauld, without his brilliancy and point.

The thing that strikes one most about Leopardi's mental attitude is the absoluteness of it. Happiness is a dream, he says, because we no sooner obtain what we wish for than it becomes repugnant to us, and we begin to long for something else. No situation is so delightful but that we can imagine another more so; and desire for that other makes the actual one wretched by comparison. But does it? Is it not possible to recognize that one might be happier, and yet be very happy at the same time?

With such beliefs as these, the natural course to take would be suicide. If life is so utterly worthless and miserable, why not get out of it? On this point

A PESSIMIST POET

Leopardi is not satisfactory. Schopenhauer treats it logically by explaining that life is, indeed, miserable, since it is the indulgence of the tyrannous Will; but to take one's life is an even more violent act of will, which, instead of freeing us, involves us only more deeply. We must emancipate ourselves by becoming indifferent to life, death, or anything else. Leopardi has not this resource. He is constantly dwelling on the superior charms of death, and charging mankind with cowardice for not seeking it; but he does not state clearly whether he is himself deterred by this consideration, or by some other. The 'Dialogue between Plotinus and Porphyrius' turns on this subject, but the arguments are neither very clear nor very strong.

The truth is that, like every one with a dogma to defend, Leopardi was blind to any consideration that did not support his position. He was not contented with being unhappy himself; he was determined that every one else should be unhappy, as well. Not, of course, that he was anxious to make them so; but he wished them to understand that they were necessarily so, and that nothing but their own folly prevented them from seeing it. Thus it was natural that he should be irritated when told that he looked at life through dark glasses, and was misled by his own physical weakness and suffering. He solemnly denies this, not seeing, apparently, that no denial of his could possibly affect the argument; unless, indeed, he had brought forward as the greatest proof that Nature was malign, her having made him to call her so. This he neglects to do; and the healthy part of mankind will, therefore, forever regard him as a melancholy hypochondriac.

Independent of his health, it is, however, clear that many circumstances combined to give him a peculiar view of things. His family relations were trying. He had constantly before him the degradation of Italy, brought home more keenly by his familiarity with the history of her past. Above all, as we have seen, he was long isolated in a provincial town, removed from the stir of modern life, which produces skepticism, but teaches toleration, comprehension of varying conditions. The results of this are everywhere seen in Leopardi, and make him seem, in spite of all his scholarship and all his literary ability, like a fretful and irritated child, who cries, as I heard one the other day: 'I'm not happy, and I haven't got anything to make me happy.' This is the whole philosophy of Leopardi.

A PESSIMIST POET

III

Leopardi was not a philosopher, but a man of letters. His work does not embody a consistent system of reasoning; but it offers us a study of human life — not, indeed, broad in its scope, yet subtle, above all passionate, and carried on with an exquisite feeling for certain kinds of beauty in style. The models that he set before himself were the Greeks and the early Italians: he sought purity and simplicity rather than the richness and variety of color that belong to a great deal of modern writing; but such means as he used were perfectly within his control, and his care and patience are shown by the great number of varying readings which have been published in recent editions of his works. This devotion to the technical part of style recalls Flaubert, with whom Leopardi has something in common; though the great French novelist had a far wider and stronger hold on human life in general.[1]

[1] An Italian critic gives some statistics as to Leopardi's style — stating, among other things, that the number of adjectives in a thousand words averages 62, taking all his poems but one — 'La Ginestra.' This is also the case with Dante's 'Divina Commedia.' Such figures have not much value, yet they are suggestive. I give some computations that I have had the curiosity to make on the English poets. In ten thousand words taken from different poems of Keats, the proportion of adjectives to the thousand is 126, in Milton, 113; in Spenser, 108. In Shakespeare it is only 63; and this is not wholly owing to Shakespeare's works being dramatic, since I find the proportion in Fletcher to be 79.

A NATURALIST OF SOULS

The love of simplicity, of pure yet energetic form, is undoubtedly what gives Leopardi his popularity in Italy, as to which Signor Piergili says: 'Does not this person know that Leopardi is one of the authors most studied among us — that he is studied and learned by heart, not only by the pupils in the schools, in the technological institutes, and in the universities, but even by young girls, who cannot pretend to more than a moderate education?' 'Amore e Morte' seems a curious study for young girls; but then — so is Shelley's 'Revolt of Islam.'

This simplicity of form also separates Leopardi from the romantic writers of his own generation in Italy, France, England, and Germany. His quiet and isolated life, his constant preoccupation with the classics, made him prize a severe and statuesque restraint much more than they did. Yet in spirit, in feeling, he was profoundly romantic; and it is just this combination that makes him interesting. His classicism was not the tawdry frippery of the eighteenth century, which injures Byron when he does not shake himself free from it; it was the same passion for clear, perfect lines that possessed Goethe; and Leopardi, with Italian to work in, was able to satisfy it better than Goethe ever succeeded in doing. But underneath the polished form lurks a fire none the less fierce for being hidden: all the restlessness, the questioning, the defiance, which Byron wore upon his sleeve for daws to peck at, Leopardi carried in his heart, wove it subtly into the fiber of his verses, to be plucked out readily enough by a sympathetic hand. I say his verses, because the personal element comes in there more clearly than in his prose. In spite of all his skill, the dialogues are tedious. They have an air of pretension which is unjustified. We look for philosophy, and get nothing but railing; not cynical indeed — there is too much earnestness for that — but cold. The writer evidently makes an effort to keep in the background. But Leopardi's poetry is personal, lyrical. It is less vehement, less incoherent, than Byron or Shelley or Obermann, but not less passionate, less sincere. Sincerity, genuineness, are, indeed, stamped on every line Leopardi wrote. His thinking may have been neither clear nor logical; but his feeling is at once subtle, thoroughly modern, and of a kind not quite to be paralleled in any contemporary literature.

Leopardi's poetry consists, besides some boyish work, of translations done in his youth, when he was busy with philology, of forty-one short pieces published in his lifetime, and of the 'Paralipomena to the Batrachomyomachia,' formerly attributed to Homer. The latter poem, which is of considerable length, is a mock-heroic, composed in Leopardi's last years to satirize contemporary political events. It is difficult for a foreigner to follow, and, moreover, attempts humor, which with Leopardi always results in a sort of skull and crossbones effect. The execution is skillful, and reminds one constantly of Ariosto — but only to bring out the difference between his joyous license and the contracted grimaces of his modern imitator.

Of the 'Canti,' or 'Odes,' the first four or five, written before their author had learned his strength, are full of patriotic rhetoric about Italy. Leopardi ostensibly kept his moral enthusiasms quite independent of his philosophical doctrines; but, nevertheless, these poems ring a little hollow. The imitation of the classics is too apparent; and it is hard to associate passion with such a frequent appeal to 'numi,' in the plural, or with such frigid encouragement as: 'But for thine own sake set thy heart upon the goal. What is life for? For nothing but that we should contemn it; it is happy only when, absorbed in perils, it forgets itself, takes no note of the filthy, tedious hours, hears not the flowing of them, happy only when with foot treading the Lethean shore it begins at last to smile.' Yet these Odes, like the later ones, have traces of the grand style about them; one is reminded everywhere of Petrarch, often of a greater than Petrarch — of the greatest of all the poets of Italy.

Such poems as those addressed to Count Carlo Pepoli or 'La Ginestra' have a general philosophical tendency resembling that of the 'Dialogues.' 'La Ginestra' is one of Leopardi's latest and longest works, written with all his simplicity, and with such Dantesque touches as —

'Quale star può quel c' ha in error la sede.'

It is the most complete exposition of his more mature philosophical views, and shows a certain abandonment of the attitude of fierce scorn for that of love and tenderness; as in the celebrated line, 'I know not which prevails, laughter or pity.' But I am inclined to think Leopardi's most devoted readers generally prefer the shorter and more lyrical pieces.

These are of two kinds; those which depict the feelings of some other person than the poet himself, or are at least general, and those which are strictly personal, and express his own experience and opinions directly. Among those of the first class we have 'The Last Song of Sappho,' 'Calm after Storm,' 'The Nocturnal Song of a Wandering Shepherd of Asia,' 'The Setting of the Moon,' 'Love and Death.' The descriptive pieces usually begin with a sketch of some scene or event, and conclude with a moral — a melancholy moral, of course. Thus, in 'Calm after Storm,' we have first the picture of peace returning to the landscape, and then the comment, quite in Leopardi's vein: 'O, courteous Nature, these are thy gifts, these the delights thou bestowest upon men. To escape from grief is a delight to us. Sorrows thou scatterest with an open hand; woe springs unsummoned; and such joy as is born rarely, a wonder and miracle, from ill, is a precious gain. The human race dear to the Gods! Happy enough are we, if we are allowed to breathe exempt from misery, blessed if death frees us from all pain.'

The quality of natural description that appears in all these poems is that of Greek and Latin poetry; it is clear, direct, simple — as, for instance, in 'The Village Saturday': 'A maiden comes from the fields at sunset with a sheaf of grain, bearing in her hand a bunch of roses and violets.' Color, the rich warmth of feeling for Nature which belongs to the northern nations, Leopardi has not. His passion is all for the interests and sufferings of man. And in these semi-dramatic poems it makes itself felt with wonderful intensity. Still it is the same refrain: 'All is mystery save our grief. Neglected offspring, we are born to tears, and the cause is hidden in the bosom of the gods.' 'This I know and feel,' sings the Shepherd of Asia, 'that from the endless flow of things, that from my frail being, some good or joy may come to others; but life is misery to me.' 'The Setting of the Moon' ends thus: 'But mortal life, when once fair youth has vanished, shines with a lovely color never more, knows no new dawn. Widowed is it till the end; and on the night which sheds its shadows over all past years the Gods have set the sepulchre for sign and seal.'

More impressive still becomes this cry of revolt and pain in the pieces where the poet speaks himself. The most common subject of lyrical outbursts, love, is not very prominent in Leopardi. Yet a number of poems touch upon it vaguely. 'Silvia' and 'The Recollection' refer to passions of his youth, 'when the harsh, unworthy mystery of things comes to us full of sweetness.' 'Aspasia' recounts a later affair, which resulted in disappointment and bitterness. He was not more fortunate in love than in other things. Here, too, he was, perhaps, led astray by the worship of an impossible ideal. The verses 'To His Lady' would form a rather perilous standard for earthly love-making: 'Naught on earth resembles thee; and if anything should seem to resemble thee in feature, in act, in speech, it would be, even so like, less beautiful than thou.'

The most interesting of these personal lyrics are those in which the poet strikes slight chords in his own remembered life, the echo of which shudders into a vague harmony of grief. Such is the poem 'To the Moon,' grand and clear as Petrarch, with its

> 'Il rimembrar delle passate cose.'

Such is 'The Infinite,' which I give in verse, reflecting, alas! but feebly the solemn beauty of the original:

> 'This tender slope was always dear to me
> And this enclosure, which shuts off my gaze
> From half the circle of the far horizon.
> And sitting here, in thought I have devised
> Interminable vastness, out beyond,
> And superhuman silence, and some rest
> Profoundest, gazing, where a little while
> The heart frets not itself. And as I hear
> The night-wind howling idly through the woods,
> I can compare its turbulence with that
> Infinity of silence, and remember

The eternal, and the years past, and those present
And passing, and their murmur. So in this
Immensity my thought has lost itself,
Nor am I loath to wreck in such a sea.'

Such is the longer 'Evening after a Festival,' describing the poet's agony at parting from his mistress, and comparing it to the fretful sorrow of a child, who, after his holiday has fled, lies oppressed with the utter, blank monotony of life:

'In my first childish years,
When some bright, longed-for, happy day had come,
And passed, and gone, I, grieving, on my couch
Lay, watched; and in the stillness of the night
A song far-heard in dark and quiet ways,
Which swelled upon the silence and died off,
Even then, as now, passionately wrung my heart.'

He to whom this does not recall a thousand things will find nothing to please him in Leopardi.

It will be sufficiently clear that Leopardi, in spite of his great originality, has a good deal in common with the Sénancours and Chateaubriands of France, the Byrons and Shelleys of England. He was an idealist, as they were. The realities of life disgusted him. His heart was fixed on a new heaven and a new earth. Only he had no sort of confidence that the ideal would ever become real. He shows not one trace of interest in the great democratic movement that began with the French Revolution. He is full of scorn for the nineteenth century, with its printing-press, its philanthropy, its calm assumption of superiority over the past: 'The wise heads of my time found out a new and almost divine plan: not being able to make any one on earth happy, forgetting individuals, they set themselves to work to seek a common happiness; and this being found easily, these people make of a race each wretched and miserable a joyous and happy nation.' Leopardi is irreligious, as were many of his French and English fellows. But his irreligion is cold and indifferent, not defiant. The gods are not to him great blighting shadows, to be combated; they are vague personifications, too insignificant to be treated even with contempt. Yet neither Shelley nor Byron nor Heine has surpassed the blank, tremendous blasphemy of Leopardi, sterner and more overwhelming because it is so cold: 'Bitter and gray is life; there is naught else but grayness and bitterness; mere slough is this world. Rest forever. Despair now for the last time. To me fate gave nothing but to die. Nature ever spurns thee — Nature, the ugly power, which rules in secret to the common ill, and the infinite vanity of things.' Yet even here one sees that the poet is led astray by the very excess of idealism in him. It is said that he was led to think all men knaves, because he was ready to trust all men. The same childish absoluteness is manifest in his writings. Every one must notice his extreme fondness for personification. This poor deity, Nature, is maltreated by him because he conceives her, not formally, but constantly, as a remote human being animated with the most anthropomorphic spite. Scherer, the French critic, notices this in his essay on Amiel: '"I know Nature is deaf," cries Leopardi, "that she thinks not of happiness, but of being only." Passion of a fretful child! Nature is neither deaf, nor preoccupied, nor cruel — she is what she is.' Taken by itself, this sounds rather oracular, but it offers just the correction Leopardi requires.

Yet it is this very absoluteness that makes him lovable. It is because his heart beats so warm with human affection that he revolts against the necessary conventionality of life; it is because he conceives so high a destiny for man that he proclaims the utter vileness of all that man has done or does. He is no skeptic, no cynic, no Epicurean. He is hopeless, but not loveless; and by that tenderness and breadth of love he has a close kinship with the great English poet who lived near him without knowing him, who sung the woes of life as clearly as Leopardi, but far more clearly the regeneration love might work, if only love would take heart and face its task.

The net result we get from Leopardi is certainly disappointing, and to most people irritating. We rebel against this positive assertion of our misery on grounds of sentiment, but still more on grounds of fact. Tell us life is wretched, if you will — perhaps even more wretched than happy; but tell us that life contains no happiness at all, and most of us answer, 'Please speak for yourself.' Life is not made on such an absolute plan. Mysterious it certainly is; but there are bright spots in it — yes, for all of us! Sainte-Beuve says, speaking of Chateaubriand, 'I know the race of René: they have their moments of unhappiness, when they cry from the housetops and pour out their miseries to the universe; they have days of joy which they bury in silence.' The insinuation of rhetoric and posing here implied does not affect Leopardi; but, though his notes of quietness and peace are rare, they occasionally come. With one of these, an appeal to Nature not as an 'ugly power,' but as the sweetest, gentlest of comforters, let me end. 'For even if life is shorn of love and all sweet dreams, even if star-

A PESSIMIST POET

less night shuts round me in the midst of spring,
yet have I my comfort and revenge lying here idle,
quiet on the grass, smiling at earth and sky and
sea.'

1893

V
ANTHONY TROLLOPE

V

ANTHONY TROLLOPE

IT is pleasant to see signs of a Trollope revival, and we may well hope that readers who are a little tired of cloak and sword romance will be glad to seek variety in the pages of 'Doctor Thorne' and the Barchester Chronicles. Perhaps no writer represents more perfectly than Trollope the great development of social and domestic tendencies in the English novel of the middle and third quarter of the last century. A man of real genius, he yet had not genius enough to stand out from and above his time; and for that very reason he portrays it more fully, just as Ben Jonson brings us nearer to the Elizabethan Age than does Shakespeare.

Trollope was essentially a realist; by which I do not mean that he had any elaborate theory as to his art, but simply that he described common life as common people see it. Realism is genius in the expression of the commonplace. Imagine a beef-eating, fox-hunting, Gaul-hating Englishman, red-cheeked, arrogant, stuffed full of prejudice, loathing a radical, idolizing a bishop and a lord, and worshiping British liberty — imagine such a one with the exceptional gift of depicting himself and many another like him to the very life, and you have the author of 'Orley Farm' and 'Phineas Finn.'

It would be desirable to reprint Trollope's Autobiography with the novels, as no novelist has left us a more entertaining and instructive account of himself and his objects and methods of work. No character in his stories stands out more distinctly before us than the awkward, unfortunate, neglected boy, who tripped and stumbled through an imperfect education and a premature manhood, a burden and annoyance to his friends, an object of disgust and dissatisfaction to himself. Nor does any novel present a happier ending to the imagination of the sympathetic reader than that pleasant picture of a way found out of difficulties, of success achieved by honest industry, of self-respecting, middle-class virtue rewarded with unlimited whist, wine, cigars, and fox-hunting. It is enough to turn the ambition of every poor boy in the direction of authorship.

What is especially delightful in Trollope's confessions is the utter absence of shame. Other artists — some others — do their pot-boiling in private, and proclaim publicly their scorn of pecuniary gain, their adoration of art for art's sake. Trollope writes for money, and is proud of getting it. He speaks of 'that high-flown doctrine of the contempt of money, which I have never admired.' If he can make a work of perfect art, well and good; but perfect or imperfect, it must sell. He gives an elaborate table — doubtless to many young authors the most interesting portion of the book — containing a full, dated list of all his writings and the sums received for each of them up to the year 1879, amounting to three hundred and fifty thousand dollars.

Nor did Trollope believe that genius must be pampered, humored, taken at its propitious times and seasons. In the nineteenth century everything should be manufactured mechanically, books as well as shoes. 'I had long since convinced myself that in such work as mine the great merit consisted in acknowledging myself to be bound by rules of labor similar to those which an artisan or a mechanic is forced to obey. A shoemaker, when he has finished one pair of shoes, does not sit down and contemplate his work in idle satisfaction: "There is my pair of shoes finished at last! What a pair of shoes it is!" The shoemaker who so indulged himself would be without wages half his time. It is the same with a professional writer of books. . . . Having thought much of all this, and having made up my mind that I could be really happy only when I was at work, I had now quite accustomed myself to begin a second pair as soon as the first was out of my hands.'

All the details of this cobbling process are complacently revealed to us. So many words an hour — 'to write with my watch before me, and to require from myself two hundred and fifty words every quarter of an hour. I have found that the two hundred and fifty words were forthcoming as regularly as my watch went' — so many hours a day, so many novels a year! Carlyle required absolute silence and leisure for production: the hand-organ over the way tormented him to fury. But this characteristic author of the nineteenth century is indifferent to time and place. 'I made for myself, therefore, a little tablet, and found, after a few days' exercise, that I could write as quickly in a railway carriage as I could at my desk.' These bits of insight into the method of production will mean more to us when we come to look more closely into the product itself.

Trollope's novels deal almost entirely with the author's own time; no mediæval history, bravos, swordplay, moonlight romance. His people are common people; that is, they are human beings like other human beings, before they are anything else. It is this constant detection of ordinary human nature under the disguises of wealth and aristocracy which misleads Mr. Saintsbury into calling Trollope a painter of middle-class life. His painting of middle-class life is good, much better than his painting of low life; but certainly his best work is on the upper classes — dukes and duchesses, earls and barons, bishops and Cabinet ministers, or, more briefly, ladies and gentlemen. Only somehow, under his quiet but penetrating insight, all these high personages, without becoming in the least vulgar or unnatural,[1] seem to drop their titles and tinsel and appear just as middling as the middlest of us. This, too, without any of those constant depreciatory remarks which so abound in Thackeray and constitute a sort of back-handed snobbishness. Trollope's great ones are simply and naturally men and women — nothing more.

So far as plot goes, in the stricter sense of the word, Trollope confesses that he is weak, and few will be found to differ from him. Sir Walter Besant's entertaining pamphlet containing a recipe for producing novels — Besant novels — has no

[1] In spite of some odd lapses of grammar and occasionally of manners, which make it seem as if Trollope himself had not always lived with dukes and bishops.

application here. The elaborate machinery of scenarii, with every motive and every climax carefully fitted into place before one line is written, does not at all suit our easy-going improvisator. 'There are usually some hours of agonizing doubt, almost of despair — so, at least, it has been with me. And then, with nothing settled in my brain as to the final development of events, with no capability of settling anything, but with a most distinct conception of some character or characters, I have rushed at the work as a rider rushes at a fence which he does not see.' And speaking of that arch-plotter of plotters, Wilkie Collins, he says: 'When I sit down to write a novel, I do not at all know and I do not very much care how it is to end. Wilkie Collins seems so to construct his that he not only, before writing, plans everything out, down to the minutest detail, from the beginning to the end; but then plots it all back again to see that there is no piece of necessary dovetailing which does not dovetail with absolute accuracy. . . . Such work gives me no pleasure. I am, however, quite prepared to admit that the want of pleasure comes from a fault of my intellect.'

Yet, although the dramatic continuity of Trollope's stories is seldom complete, we constantly

come across those intensely effective and striking
scenes which are perhaps the best thing in a good
novel, which we pause to read twice over, which
cling in the memory and keep returning to us, yet
are always fresh and delightful when we come to
them again. Mr. Slope's slap in the face and his
fierce fight with Mrs. Proudie for the domination
of the Bishop, the pitched battle between Mrs.
Proudie and Mrs. Grantly, the delicious scene between Lady Lufton and Lucy Roberts, and the
somewhat similar one between the Archdeacon and
Grace Crawley, Johnny Eames and the bull, Lord
Chiltern riding Dandolo, Madame Max and the
Duchess over the jewels, Phineas's acquittal —
these are but a tithe of what lovers of Trollope will
take joy in recalling.

The life of such scenes comes from the ever-
present and admirably sustained interest of character, and this interest gives to Trollope's novels a
unity which is wanting in their plots. One can
never insist too much on the immense superiority of
English literature in general over all others in this
point of character. Richness and fullness of human
life are what distinguish the drama of Shakespeare
from that of Sophocles, of Calderon, of Racine, of
Dumas *fils*. An excellence of the same kind, un-

usual in French writers, but far inferior not only to Shakespeare's, but to Jonson's or Fletcher's or Massinger's, gives Molière his great reputation. So in the novel. French fiction may surpass English in skill of construction, in finished elegance of style, in grace and charm. It never approaches it in fertility, variety, and strength of character production. One has only to compare Dumas with Scott, George Sand with George Eliot, to feel the force of this. Balzac, like Molière, is great because he is an exception; but, like Molière, he accomplishes with Titanic effort what Shakespeare, Fielding, Miss Austen, Thackeray, and Dickens do with divine ease and unerring instinct. With a great price bought he this freedom, but they were born free.

Without placing Trollope on a level with these greatest masters, it is easy to see that with him also character is a strong point. He always recognizes this himself, and in his Autobiography he has some admirable observations on the subject in connection with the sensational in novels. Speaking of 'The Bride of Lammermoor,' of 'Esmond,' of 'Jane Eyre,' he says: 'These stories charm us, not simply because they are tragic, but because we feel that men and women with flesh and blood, creatures with whom we can sympathize, are struggling amid their woes. It all lies in that. No novel is anything, for the purposes either of comedy or tragedy, unless the reader can sympathize with the characters whose names he finds upon the pages. . . . Truth let there be, truth of description, truth of character, human truth as to men and women. If there be such truth, I do not know that a novel can be too sensational.'

From the very fact of pitching his characters so largely on a middle note, of choosing them and keeping them always in the common light of every day, Trollope gives peculiarly the impression of having lived with them and of making us live with them. He often goes into very diffuse analyses of the thought and actions of his heroes and heroines; yet in so doing he does not seem to sap their vitality as do Thackeray and George Eliot. The reason of this is that he does not appear to be explaining, but speculating. He does not say, 'I made this machine, and I can tell you just how it goes.' He talks to you as a friend would talk about another friend in a desultory, twilight chat, before a smouldering fire. His characters seem to exist entirely independent of their author, and to work out their own natures with no volition or even control from him.

A NATURALIST OF SOULS

This is doubtless one of the advantages of his rapid and instinctive method of working.

This common naturalness of Trollope's characters, this feeling that we have lived with them and known them, is much intensified by their constant reappearance in different stories. Of course, many other authors have held their characters along from one book to another; but neither Dumas nor Balzac nor Mr. Howells has done it to the same extent as Trollope. He speaks somewhere of his lack of memory; but surely a memory approaching instinct was needed to carry a company of people through thirty-two volumes,[1] with long intervals of time both in the subjects and in the composition, and to keep constantly a distinct grasp not only of general traits of character, but of eyes and hair, of gait and gesture. In this vast and loose sequence of events and circumstances slips and inaccuracies doubtless occur, but their rarity is wonderful.

In such a crowd of characters we can hardly

[1] It may interest some of Trollope's admirers to have a complete list of the long series of connected novels which include most of his best work. The six chronicles of Barset come first as follows: *The Warden, Barchester Towers, Doctor Thorne, Framley Parsonage, The Small House at Allington, The Last Chronicle of Barset.* These are followed by the parliamentary novels, the connection between them being maintained through Mr. Palliser and some others: *Can You Forgive Her?, Phineas Finn, The Eustace Diamonds, Phineas Redux, The Prime Minister, The Duke's Children.*

single out many for special consideration. Mr. Saintsbury, who has written of Trollope with sympathy and appreciation, speaks of Mr. Crawley as almost the only one of his personages who stands out with real originality and permanent significance, and Trollope himself has an unusual affection for that eccentric gentleman; but Mr. Crawley is too exceptional, too near the limits of sanity, for the deepest human interest. How inferior he is to the Archdeacon, the admirable Archdeacon, at once perfect (artistically perfect) man and perfect English clergyman! How we love him, with his conventional dignity, his conventional religion, his bustling meddlesomeness, his tyrannous impertinence, his sturdy English common sense, his never-failing ejaculation, 'Good Heavens!' — how we love him! And in a far different fashion how we love Mr. Harding, one of the tenderest, simplest, most touching figures in fiction, whose gentle memory brings the tears to one's eyes! How we should delight, unobserved, to watch him in one of the stalls of his beloved cathedral choir, turning over the pages of his own church music, gently and absently playing seraphic airs on an imaginary violoncello!

'Heard melodies are sweet, but those unheard
Are sweeter.'

Mr. Harding, perhaps the most striking of all Trollope's creations, because so totally unlike Trollope himself, whereas the Archdeacon is clearly the very image of the author of his being.

Then the women — Mrs. Proudie — we all detest her. Yet we have a sneaking fondness for her, too. There is one of the marks of large humanness in Trollope: he brings out something not wholly hateful in the worst character he touches. The masters of human life in literature, Shakespeare and Scott, have the same trait. And Lady Glencora — how well we know her, and who does not feel her fascination! Trollope's own observations on her show how far a true artist's judgment may be below his genius: 'She has, or has been intended to have, beneath the thin stratum of her follies a basis of good principle, which enabled her to live down the original wrong that was done to her, and taught her to endeavor to do her duty in the position to which she was called.' And this is Lady Glen — the sprightly, the mobile, the petulant, the willful, the bewitching Lady Glen! It would be instructive if we had the original skeletons of Rosalind and Diana Vernon to range and ticket on the same shelf with this inert anatomy.

Nor is it only in what dramatic slang would call

'character parts' that Trollope succeeds. In the still more difficult task of giving individual life to heroes and heroines he shows himself equally skillful. Phineas Finn, for example, is intended to be and is a very ordinary person; yet an indescribable and indefinable something of lovableness pervades his character everywhere, so that one cannot choose but love him. As for Trollope's girls — Eleanor Harding, Mary Thorne, Lucy Roberts, Lily Dale, Grace Crawley, Violet Effingham, Isabel Boncassen, and the rest — they are charming, and at the same time they are remarkably distinct: each keeps her individuality in the midst of the general fascination.

The style in which Trollope writes about all these personages is what might be expected from the author's method of working — loose, free, easily followed. After all, perhaps this is the best style for story-telling, when a man has the gift of it. The curious felicity of Flaubert and Stevenson is a precious thing; but one never escapes the sense that it is born of painful effort, and one feels a little guilty not to enjoy it with a certain effort also. The Goncourts speak somewhere of the struggle with which an author tears forth a beautiful page from his very vitals. Trollope never tore any pages from his vitals; he had no vitals, literarily speaking. Easy, rapid, graceful improvisation, at the rate of a thousand words an hour, as aforesaid, was good enough for him — and for most of his readers. Gautier said that the production of copy was a natural function with George Sand. So it was with Trollope: he wrote as easily as he breathed — or hunted — yet his style is full of individuality. It has neither dignity nor power nor remarkable precision; but it has a peculiar homely, personal flavor, as of a man loosely noting his natural thought, writing in old clothes, with a pipe in his mouth and a glass of old wine beside him. The very tricks of it — that most marked one, which Mr. Saintsbury has noted, of repeating and emphasizing words — are characteristic of the man, and one gets attached to them as to him.

As for observation, Trollope had little, so far as the external world is concerned; but his moral insight is close and keen on the somewhat superficial plane to which he was limited by nature. 'That which enables the avaricious and unjust to pass scatheless through the world is not the ignorance of the world as to their sins, but the indifference of the world as to whether they be sinful or no.' 'The little sacrifices of society are all made by women as are also the great sacrifices of life. A man who is good for anything is always ready for his duty, and so is a good woman for her sacrifice.' 'Men are cowards before women till they become tyrants.' 'Why is it that girls so constantly do this? So frequently ask men who have loved them to be present at their marriages with other men? There is no triumph in it; it is done in sheer kindness and affection. "You can't marry me yourself," the lady seems to say, "but the next greatest blessing I can offer you, you shall have: you shall see me married to somebody else." I fully appreciate the intention, but in all honesty I doubt the eligibility of the proffered entertainment.'

The last quotation shows the sort of good-natured satire which keeps one smiling through a great part of Trollope's work. Mr. Howells, in his otherwise most appreciative criticism, charges Trollope with a lack of humor. To most of Trollope's admirers it seems that his novels are full of humor; not indeed overcharged and farcical, like Dickens's, always restrained within the limits of nature, but true humor nevertheless.

I have said nothing as yet, however, of that which constitutes the greatest claim of Trollope's novels to permanence; I mean, their picture of contemporary English life. Even where plot and character are weakest, there is always something of vitality and truth, and so of interest, in the background and surroundings; but when we come to the Barchester and Parliamentary series, the richness and accuracy of detail are wonderful. Every syllable that deals with Barchester has the accent of truth. I have already referred to Archdeacon Grantly, who is so clerical and so English as well as so human; but all his surroundings, the bishops and the deans and canons, and the wives of these dignitaries and their very children, and all that they say and do, bring the quaint, quiet air of the cathedral town about us. Surely future ages will turn to Trollope more than to any other author for a true and vivid picture of this life, when it shall have wholly passed away.

The Parliamentary atmosphere is naturally less peculiar in its interest, but its appeal is stronger on that very account. We know by Trollope's own confession that he failed to obtain a seat in the House of Commons. We know from the same source that to obtain such a seat was one of the ambitions of his life. It does not seem possible that if he had obtained it he could have acquired a more intimate knowledge of the details of Parliamentary practice. Certainly no formal history could give us half the insight into the machinery of government that we get from him. All the technicalities of majorities, cabinets, readings, questions, committees, whips, and the rest of it, all the ins and outs of candidacies, elections, ballotings with eggthrowing accompaniment, take life and significance from the human figures with which they are associated, and in turn give to these human figures a body and a substance which would otherwise be lacking.

Then the hunting — oh, the hunting! I have referred to it before, but it is worth mentioning ten times over. Unquestionably it is the best part of Trollope. Others have described it from the desk and the chimney corner; but he gives it fresh from the field, crisp with the hoarfrost of the autumn morning, glowing with the very rush and ardor of the thing itself. Oh, the deep voice of the hounds, and the red coats flashing, and the stride of the steeds, and the thick of the hurly-burly! It is dragged into novel after novel, as Trollope himself admits; yet the novels that are without it seem by comparison to be only half alive.

With this note of external, physical life and activity it is well to leave Trollope. As I said in the beginning, he is a true realist, a common man giving the views and the feelings of common men. His moral attitude is always proper and decent, sometimes even to the extent of sermonizing; but he has no spiritual ideal, no sense of passionate moral struggle, no aspiration after the unseen and the divine. Stuffed full of British conventions, he is, and will remain, the loyal interpreter of British — and other — Philistinism, all the more loyal because instinctive and unconscious. What Philistine would not die happy if he could sum up his career in the following paragraph? 'If the rustle of a woman's petticoat has ever stirred my blood, if a cup of wine has been a joy to me, if I have thought tobacco at midnight in pleasant company to be one of the elements of an earthly paradise, if now and again I have somewhat recklessly fluttered a five-pound note over a card table, of what matter is it to any reader? I have betrayed no woman. Wine has brought me to no sorrow. It has been the companionship of smoking that I have loved rather than the habit. I have never desired to win money, and I have lost none. To enjoy the excitement of pleasure, but to be free from its vices and evil effects, to have the sweet and leave the bitter untasted — that has been my study. The preachers tell us that this is impossible. It seems to me that I have succeeded fairly well.'

1901

VI
AN ODD SORT OF POPULAR BOOK

VI

AN ODD SORT OF POPULAR BOOK

MULTIPLICITY of editions does not make a book a classic. Otherwise Worcester's Dictionary and Mrs. Lincoln's Cook-Book might almost rival Shakespeare. Nevertheless, when a work, which has little but its literary quality to recommend it, achieves sudden and permanent popularity, it is safe to assume that there is something about it which will repay curious consideration. As to the popularity of 'The Anatomy of Melancholy,' there can be no dispute. 'Scarce any book of philology in our land hath, on so short a time, passed through so many editions,' says old Fuller. The first of these editions appeared in 1621. It was followed by four others during the few years preceding the author's death in 1640. Three more editions were published at different times in the seventeenth century. The eighteenth century was apparently contented to read Burton in the folios; but the book was reprinted in the year 1800, and since then it has been issued in various forms at least as many as forty times, though never as yet with what might be called thorough editing.

Quantity of approval is in this case well supported by quality. Milton showed his admiration, as usual, by imitation. Sterne conveyed passage after passage almost bodily into 'Tristram Shandy.' Southey's odd book, 'The Doctor,' follows Burton closely in manner and often in matter. Dr. Johnson said that 'The Anatomy of Melancholy' was the only book that ever took him out of bed two hours sooner than he wished to rise; large commendation surely, and I have never found any other, even of the most devout Burtonians, quite ready to echo it. Lamb was a reader, adorer, and imitator; Keats, the first two, at any rate. Finally, Mr. Saintsbury assures us that 'for reading either continuous or desultory, either grave or gay, at all times of life and in all moods of temper, there are few authors who stand the test of practice so well as the author of "The Anatomy of Melancholy."' For all that, I would not advise the general reader to buy a copy in too great haste. He will, perhaps, find it easier to read about the book than to read it.

What we know of the life of Robert Burton is a very small matter, as is the case with so many of his greater contemporaries. He was born at Lindley in Leicestershire, in 1577, thirteen years after Shakespeare, four years after Ben Jonson. He was at School at Sutton-Coldfield, in Warwickshire, and at Nuneaton, till he was seventeen. He then went to Brasenose College. In 1599 he was elected student of Christ Church. In 1614 he received the degree of B.D., and in 1616, he became vicar of Saint Thomas, in the west suburb of Oxford. About 1636 he added to this cure the rectory of Segrave in Leicestershire. Besides 'The Anatomy' he wrote a Latin comedy, 'Philosophaster,' unusually clever and brilliant in its kind. He died in 1640, and was buried in the choir of Christ Church Cathedral. The little bit of gossip narrated by Wood is amusingly illustrative of the mythical character so apt to attach itself to the solitary scholar. It seems that Burton's death occurred at or very near the time which had been foretold by himself from the calculation of his own nativity; in consequence of which 'several of the students did not forbear to whisper among themselves that, rather than there should be a mistake in the calculation, he sent up his soul to heaven through a slip about his neck.' With the exception of a few other scraps of doubtful hearsay and of the full text of his will, this is all of importance that has come down to us about the author of 'The Anatomy.' It is rather brief, when one realizes that, if he had lived two hundred and fifty years later, he would probably have been honored with two solid volumes of so-called biography, like many another much less worthy of it.

Far more than most great writers, however, Burton left the reflection of his life and character in his work, and 'The Anatomy of Melancholy' may be called one of the most intensely personal books ever written. To be sure, the author does not constantly and directly refer to himself and his own affairs. Nevertheless, the impress of his spirit is felt on every page.

Several of the biographical facts above mentioned are derived from casual remarks dropped here and there throughout the book. Of his mother, Mistress Dorothy Burton, he says that she had 'excellent skill in Chirurgery, sore eyes, aches, etc.,' and that she had 'done many famous and good cures upon divers poor folks that were otherwise destitute of help.' He gives us a reminiscence of his boyhood: 'They think no slavery in the world (as once I did myself) like to that of a grammar scholar.' He speaks with a grain of bitterness of a younger brother's lot: 'I do much respect and honour true gentry and nobility; I was born of worshipful parents myself, in an ancient family; but I am a younger brother, it concerns me not.'

He gives us many glimpses of his lonely scholar's life. In his youth he was ambitious: 'I was once so mad to bustle abroad and seek about for preferment, tire myself, and trouble all my friends.' But the world is cold, friendship formal and touches not the heart: 'I have had some such noble friends, acquaintances, and scholars, but most part they and I parted as we met; they gave me as much as I requested and that was —.' His habits are those of the recluse and ascetic: 'I am a bachelor myself and lead a monastic life in college.' 'I am *aquæ potor*, drink no wine at all.' Yet he loves the sweet of nature, too, if the bitter thirst of knowledge would permit: 'No man ever took more delight in springs, woods, groves, gardens, walks, fishponds, rivers, etc.' Force of circumstance, lack of opportunity, younger brotherhood, timidity, have kept him secluded within the walls of great libraries, have piled huge dusty tomes upon the human beating of his heart. 'I have lived a silent, sedentary, solitary, private life in the University, as long almost as Xenocrates in Athens, to learn wisdom as he did, penned up most part in my study.' Yet if the Fates had willed otherwise, the man would have been consenting. Let us note right here that this is the whole charm of Burton and his great book. It is no dry treatise of a gray-haired pedant, thumbing contentedly forever dull volumes of mouldy tradition. For all its quaint garb and thorny aspect it is a great human document, the work of a man whose bodily life was passed in his study, but whose senses were all keenly, pantingly alert to catch the motion of the wide world beyond. Beauty — he adores beauty. 'This amazing, confounding, admirable beauty; 'tis nature's crown, gold, and glory.' Love — Oh, how he could have loved! 'I confess I am but a novice, a contemplator only,' he writes of it; 'yet *homo sum*, I am a man, and not altogether inexpert in this subject.' Like Flaubert, he doubtless leaned forth from his study window on many a moonlit night, and heard a company of revelers with merry song and pleasant jest, and caught the dim flutter of a white gown, and found all his books and learning mere dust beside the laughter and the passion of the world.

And so he grew melancholy, as often happens in such cases. When a man gets these fits on him, he may either rush out into active life for the sake of contrast, he may marry, or go into politics, or do something even more rash and criminal; or he may cut his throat; or he may write a book. On the whole, the last method is the most to be recommended. Burton adopted it; and, with homœo-pathic ingenuity, he wrote a book on melancholy itself. 'I write against melancholy, by being busy to avoid melancholy. . . . Shall I say, my mistress melancholy, my Egeria, or my evil genius?'

The loose and literary sense in which Burton uses the word 'melancholy' is characteristic of the tone of his book. Without really attempting any precise definition, or, rather, having confused the reader with a multitude of definitions taken from all the authors under the sun, he proceeds to include every form of nervous depression, from a mere temporary fit of the blues to acute or chronic mania and insanity. At the same time, being a man of logical and systematic turn of mind, he imposes on others, and perhaps on himself, with a great show of formal and scientific treatment. The work is mapped out into divisions, partitions, sections, members, subsections, arranged in as awful order of deduction as Euclid or the Ethics of Spinoza. But let no one be alarmed. This is pure matter of form. The author speaks of what he likes, when he likes. Occasionally he takes the pains to recognize that he is digressing, as in the delicious chapters entitled, 'A Digression of Spirits,' 'A Digression of Air.' And then, with a sigh, he tries to call himself back to the work in hand. 'But my melancholy spaniels quest, my game is sprung, and I must suddenly come down and follow.' The game leads him into strange places, however. The vast and checkered meadow of the human heart is his hunting-ground. Melancholy is the skeleton in the closet, always popping out at odd times and in unexpected corners; but he keeps it wreathed with bright flowers, and made sweet with strange and subtle savors, and brilliant and sparkling with jewels of quaint wit and wandering fancy. Nevertheless, when he does discuss his subject itself, he has bits of sound common sense, useful to-day and always, like his recommendation of 'the three Salernitan Doctors, D. Merryman, D. Diet, and D. Quiet, which cure all diseases.'

Some one may object that this saying is quoted, and not Burton's own invention. Certainly, Burton is the greatest quoter in literature, far surpassing even Montaigne. His mind was full of the thoughts of others, and he poured them forth together with his own in inextricable mixture. He was a man drenched, drowned in learning, not learning of the quick, smart, practical, modern type, which enables its possessor to give interviews on the inhabitants of Mars and testify on poisons at a murder trial, but mediæval learning, drowsy, strange, unprofit-able, and altogether lovely. In the discussion of these melancholy matters all preceding literature is laid under contribution, not only the classics, but countless writers of the Middle Ages, doubtless respectable in their own day and possibly in Bur-ton's, but now so dead that the reader stares and gasps at them and wonders whether his author is not inventing references, like the 'Oracle' in 'The Innocents Abroad.' Melanelius, Rufus, Ætius, describe melancholy 'to be a bad and peevish dis-ease.' Hercules de Saxonia approves this opinion, as do Fuchsius, Arnoldus, Guianerius, and others — not unnaturally. Paulus takes a different view, and Halyabbas still another. Aretæus calls it 'a perpetual anguish of the soul, fastened on one thing without an ague.' In this brilliant but hazy state-ment the absence of ague is at least a comfort. It is disquieting, indeed, to find that 'this definition of his Merrialis taxeth'; but we are reassured by the solid support of Œlianus Montaltus. And so on.

Pure pedantry, you will say. Well, yes. It would be, if Burton were not saved from the ex-treme of pedantry by a touch of humor, which makes you somehow feel that he does not take all this quite seriously himself. Yet it is very hard for him to look at anything except through the eyes of some remote authority. We have heard him speak of his mother's excellent cures. It seems that one of her favorite remedies was 'an amulet of a spider in a nutshell lapped in silk,' super-sovereign for the ague. Burton finds it hard to swallow this; it was 'most absurd and ridiculous; for what has a spider to do with a fever?' Ah, but one day 'rambling amongst authors (as often I do) I found this very medicine in Dioscorides, approved by Matthiolus, repeated by Aldrovandus. . . . I began to have a better opinion of it, and to give more credit to amulets.' I can see from here Mistress Dorothy Burton's lovely scorn at being confirmed by Dioscorides. What did she care for Dioscorides? Did she not have the recipe from her great-aunt, and has she not proved it a dozen times herself?

This trick of constant quoting has led some shallow people to set Burton down as a mere quoter and nothing else. There could be no greater mistake. It is the activity and independence of his own mind which make him so eager to watch and compare the minds of others; and while he profited by their thinking, he was abundantly able to do his own, as every page of his book shows. One need ask no better specimen of strong, shrewd, satirical reflection than the sketch of a Utopian commonwealth in the introduction which purports to be by Democritus, Junior; and of many other passages we may say the same.

Nor was our author lacking in deep, human sympathy, although his solitary life and keen intellect disposed him to be a trifle cynical. The celebrated bit with the refrain 'Ride on!' — so brilliantly imitated by Sterne — shows a pitiful appreciation of sorrow and misery, which, indeed, are abundantly recognized everywhere in 'The Anatomy.'

But perhaps the most characteristic illustration of Burton's intense appetite for humanity is his frequent reference to common daily life and manners. M. Anatole France tells us that the author of the 'Imitation' must certainly have been a man of the world before he betook himself to his lonely cell and pious meditation. If Burton never was a man of the world, he would certainly have liked to be one. He peers out from behind the bars of his retreat and catches every possible glimpse of the curious things which are shut away from him. Shreds of fashion, hints of frivolity, quips of courtiers, the flash of swords and glittering of jewels — he will find a place for them. Woman fascinates him especially — that singular creature who apparently cares nothing for books and study, laughs, weeps, scolds, caresses, without any reasonable cause whatever. Certainly no philosopher should take any notice of her — yet they all do. And he exhausts himself in cunning heaps of observation, vain interrogations of mysterious boudoirs: 'Why do they make such glorious shows with their scarfs, feathers, fans, masks, furs, laces, tiffanies, ruffs, falls, calls, cuffs, damasks, velvets, tinsel, cloth of gold, silver, tissue? With colors of heavens, stars, planets; the strength of metals, stones, odors, flowers, birds, beasts, fishes, and whatsoever Africa, Asia, America, sea, land, art and industry of man can afford? Why do they use such novelty of inventions; such new-fangled tires; and spend such inestimable sums on them? ... Why is it but, as a day-net catcheth larks, to make young men stoop unto them?' And old philosophers also, he might have added.

I have taken this passage from the section on 'Love Melancholy'; for Burton devotes a large portion of his work to that delightful subject. He feels it necessary to make some apology for entering upon it. Some persons will think it hardly becoming in so grave, reverend, and dignified a gentleman — a clergyman, too. But he has good authors on his side: 'I excuse myself with Peter Godefridus, Valleriola, Ficinus, Langius, Cadmus, Milesius, who writ fourteen books of love.' Surely, he would be very critical who should ask more than this.

The apology once made, with what gusto he sets forth, how he luxuriates in golden tidbits from love's delicate revels! 'A little soft hand, pretty little mouth, small, fine, long fingers, 'tis that which Apollo did admire in Daphne.' 'Of all eyes (by the way) black are most amiable, enticing, and fair.' 'Oh, that pretty tone, her divine and lovely looks, her everything lovely, sweet, amiable, and pretty, pretty, pretty.' Is it not the mere ecstasy of amorous frenzy? Again, he gives us a very banquet, a rosy wreath of old, simple English names, a perfect old-fashioned garden: 'Modest Matilda, pretty, pleasing Peg, sweet, singing Susan, mincing merry Moll, dainty dancing Doll, neat Nancy, jolly Jane, nimble Nell, kissing Kate, bouncing Bess with black eyes, fair Phillis with fine white hands, fiddling Frank, tall Tib, slender Sib, etc.' Do you not hear their merry laughter, as he heard it in his dim study, a dream of fair faces and bright forms twisting, and turning, and flashing back and forth under the harvest moon?

Yet, after all, love is a tyrant and a traitor, a

meteor rushing with blind fury among the placid orbs of life. What is a man to make of these wild contrasts and tragical transitions? At one moment the lover seems to be on the pinnacle of felicity, 'his soul soused, imparadised, imprisoned in his lady; he can do nothing, think of nothing but her; she is his cynosure, Hesperus, and Vesper, his morning and evening star, his goddess, his mistress, his life, his soul, his everything; dreaming, waking, she is always in his mouth; his heart, eyes, ears, and all his thoughts are full of her.' But then something goes wrong and the note is altogether changed. 'When this young gallant is crossed in his love, he laments, and cries, and roars downright. "The virgin's gone and I am gone, she's gone, she's gone, and what shall I do? Where shall I find her? whom shall I ask? What will become of me? I am weary of this life, sick, mad, and desperate."'

It becomes the sage, then, to be clear of these toys. If he is to write about Love Melancholy, let him cure it. Let him hold up a warning to the unwary. What is the use of days and nights spent in toiling over learned authors, if the young and foolish are not to have the benefit of one's experience? If only the young and foolish would profit! If only the unwary would beware! Still, we must do our

part. Let us remind them that beauty fades. It is a
rather well-known fact, but youth is so prone to
forget it. 'Suppose thou beholdest her in a frosty
morning, in cold weather, in some passion or perturbation of mind, weeping, chafing, etc., rivelled
and ill-favored to behold.... Let her use all helps
art and nature can yield; be like her, and her, and
whom thou wilt, or all these in one; a little sickness,
a fever, smallpox, wound, scar, loss of an eye or
limb, a violent passion, mars all in an instant, dis-
figures all.' Then let us exalt the charms of a
bachelor's life. It has its weak points, as I feel,
writing here alone in the dust and chill, with nothing but books about me, no prattle of children,
no merry chatter of busy women. But what then?
It is quieter, after all. 'Consider how contentedly,
quietly, neatly, plentifully, sweetly, and how mer-
rily he lives! He hath no man to care for but himself, none to please, no charge, none to control him,
is tied to no residence, no cure to serve, may go and
come when, whither, live where he will, his own
master, and do what he list himself.' Nevertheless,
it all sounds a little hollow, and as I sit here in the
winter midnight with my old pipe, I wonder if it
might not have been otherwise.

I have made my quotations with very small

skill, if the ingenious reader does not by this time feel that Burton was in his way a great master of style. His skill and power as a writer, more than anything else, show that he was not a mere pedant or Dryasdust. It is true, he himself disclaims any such futile preoccupation. He has not 'amended the style which now flows remissly, as it was first conceived.' His book is 'writ with as small deliberation as I do ordinarily speak, without all affectation of big words, fustian phrases, jingling terms.' But the facts belie him, and one shudders to think what must have been his idea of the big words he does not use. A careful collation of the first edition of the Anatomy with the last published in the author's lifetime not only shows a great number of additions and alterations, but proves conclusively that these changes were made, in many cases, with a view to style and to style only. Take a single instance. In the first edition Burton wrote: 'If it be so that the earth is a moon, then are we all lunatic within.' Later he amplified this as follows, with obvious gain in the beauty of the phrase: 'If it be so that the earth is a moon, then we are also giddy, vertiginous and lunatic within this sublunary maze.' Amended I think, but oh, for the 'big words, fustian phrases, jingling terms'!

Yes, Burton was a master of style. He could bend language to his ends and do as he willed with it. If he is often rough, harsh, wanton in expression, it is simply because, like Donne, he chose to be so. Does he wish to tell a plain story? Who can do it more lightly, simply, briefly? 'An ass and a mule went laden over a brook, the one with salt, the other with wool; the mule's pack was wet by chance; the salt melted, his burden the lighter; and he thereby much eased. He told the ass, who, thinking to speed as well, wet his pack likewise at the next water; but it was much the heavier, he quite tired.'

Does he wish to paint the foul and horrible? I know of nothing in Swift or Zola more replete with the luxury of hideousness than the unquotable description of the defects which infatuated love will overlook — a description which Keats tells a correspondent he would give his favorite leg to have written. Here, as in so many passages I have quoted, Burton piles up epithet after epithet, till it seems as if the dictionary would be exhausted — a trick which, by the bye, he may have caught from Rabelais, and which would become very monotonous, if it were not applied with such wonderful variety and fertility.

Then, at his will, the magician can turn with ease from the bitter to the sweet. When he touches love or beauty, all his ruggedness is gone. His words become full of grace, of suave, vague richness, of delicacy, of mystery, as in the phrase which Southey quotes in 'The Doctor': 'For peregrination charms our senses with such unspeakable and sweet variety that some count him unhappy that never traveled, a kind of prisoner, and pity his case, that from his cradle to his old age beholds the same still: still, still the same, the same.' Or, to take a more elaborate picture, see this, which might be a Tintoretto or a Spenser: 'Witty Lucian, in that pathetical love-passage or pleasant description of Jupiter's stealing of Europa and swimming from Phœnicia to Crete, makes the sea calm, the winds hush, Neptune and Amphitrite riding in their chariot to break the waves before them, the Tritons dancing round about with every one a torch; the sea-nymphs, half-naked, keeping time on dolphins' backs and singing Hymenæus; Cupid nimbly tripping on the top of the waters; and Venus herself coming after in a shell, strewing roses and flowers on their heads.'

I have dwelt thus long on Burton's style because it is absolutely characteristic, and because it proves by its eminent artistic qualities that he was not simply a compiler and quoter, but a thinking and feeling man, a strong, shrewd, passionate temperament, gazing with intense interest out of his scholastic windows at the strange and moving spectacle of life. In his fullness and abundance he, more than any other English author, recalls Montaigne, whom he occasionally quotes: he has less fluidity, more conventional prejudice, but also more sincerity, more robust moral force. Again, he in a certain sense resembles a greater than Montaigne, his own greatest contemporary, Shakespeare, whom he also quotes enough to show that he knew and loved his writings, at any rate, if not himself. Shakespeare's work is like a glorious piece of tapestry, a world of rich and splendid hues, woven into a thousand shapes of curious life. Burton's is like the reverse side of the same; all the bewildering wealth of color, but rough, crude, misshapen, undigested.

One of the characteristic oddities of Burton's style is his perpetual use of the phrase 'etc.' When his quick and fluent pen has heaped together all the nouns or adjectives in heaven, and in earth, and in the waters under the earth, he completes the picture with the vast vague gesture of an 'etc.' Take an often-quoted passage in the introduction, in which he describes his own life as an observer and contemplator: 'now come tidings of weddings, masking, mummeries, entertainments, jubilees, embassies, tilts and tournaments, trophies, triumphs, revels, sports, plays; then again, as in a new-shifted scene, treasons, cheating tricks, robberies, enormous villainies in all kinds, funerals, burials, death of princes, new discoveries, expeditions, now comical, then tragical matters; to-day we hear of new lords and officers created, to-morrow of some great men deposed, and again of fresh honors conferred; one is let loose, another imprisoned; one purchaseth, another breaketh; he thrives, his neighbor turns bankrupt; now plenty, then again dearth and famine; one runs, another rides, wrangles, laughs, weeps, etc.'

So we may sum up 'The Anatomy of Melancholy' in an 'etc.' The general tone of the book, with its infinite multiplicity, reminds one of nothing more than of the quaint blending of mirth, mystery, and spiritual awe, so deliciously expressed in Stevenson's baby couplet,

> 'The world is so full of a number of things,
> I'm sure we should all be as happy as kings.'

Only Burton would have laid a mischievous and melancholy emphasis on 'should.'

1902

VII
ALEXANDRE DUMAS

VII
ALEXANDRE DUMAS

MR. DAVIDSON, whose excellent volume on Dumas must be the foundation of any careful study of the subject, dismisses his author with the remark: 'Except for increasing the already ample means of relaxation, he did nothing to benefit humanity at large.' Is not this a rather grudging epitaph for the creator of 'Monte Cristo'? Are the means of relaxation so ample that we can afford to treat 'La Tour de Nesle' and 'La Reine Margot' as alms for oblivion? Would Stevenson have read 'Le Vicomte de Bragelonne' six times, would you or I have read 'Les Trois Mousquetaires' more times than we can count, if other relaxation of an equally delightful order were indeed so easily obtainable? In spite of the flood of historical novels and all other kinds of novels that overwhelmed the nineteenth century, story-tellers like Dumas are not born every day, nor yet every other day.

For he was a story-teller by nature, one who could make a story of anything, one who did make a story of everything, for the joy of his own child-like imagination. 'I am not like other people.

A NATURALIST OF SOULS

Everything interests me.' The round oath of a man, the smile of a woman, a dog asleep in the sun, a bird singing in a bush, even a feather floating in the breeze, was enough. Fancy seized it and wove an airy, sunbright web about it, glittering with wit, touched with just a hint of pathos; and as we read, we forget the slightness of the substance in the grace and delicacy of the texture.

It is an odd thing, this national French gift of story-telling, of seeking by instinct the group-effect, as it were, of a set of characters, their composite relations to one another and the development of these relations in dramatic climax. English writers, from Chaucer down, dwell by preference on the individual character, force it only with labor and difficulty into the general framework, from which it constantly escapes in delightful but wholly undramatic human eccentricity. To the French habit of mind, such individuality is excrescent and distasteful. Let the characters develop as fully and freely as the action requires, no more. They are there for the action, not the action for them. Hence, as the English defect is dull diffusion and a chaos of disorder, so the French is loss of human truth in a mad eagerness for forcible situations, that is to say, melodrama.

ALEXANDRE DUMAS

Even in Hugo, in Balzac, in Flaubert, in Zola, one has an uneasy feeling that melodrama is not too far away. In Dumas it is frankly present always. The situation — something that shall tear the nerves, make the heart leap and the breath stop — for Dumas there lies the true art of dramatist and novelist. And what situations! No one ever had more than he the two great dramatic gifts, which perhaps are only one, the gift of preparation and the gift of climax. 'Of all *dénouements*, past, present, and I will say even to come,' writes Sarcey, 'that of "Antony" is the most brilliant, the most startling, the most logical, the most rapid; a stroke of genius.' 'Henri III,' 'Richard Darlington,' 'La Tour de Nesle' are full of effects scarcely inferior. If one thinks first of the plays, it is only because in them the action is more concentrated than in the novels. But in novel after novel also, there is the same sure instinct of arrangement, the same masterly hand, masterly for obtaining the sort of effect which the author has chiefly in view.

And perhaps the melodrama is not quite all. The creatures are not always mere puppets, wire-pulled, stirring the pulse when they clash together, then forgotten. We hate them sometimes, sometimes love them, sometimes even remember them. Marguerite and Buridan are not wholly unreal in their wild passion. The scene of reconciliation between the Musketeers in the Place Royale has something deeper than mere effect. And these are only two among many. Under all his gift of technique, his love of startling and amazing, the man was not without an eye, a grip on life, above all, a heart that beat widely, with many sorrows and many joys.

Then the style is the style of melodrama, but it is also far more. No one knew better how and when to let loose sharp, stinging, burning shafts of phrase like the final speech of Antony, '*Elle m'a résisté; je l'ai assassinée,*' — shafts which flew over the footlights straight to the heart of every auditor. But these effects would be nothing without the varied movement of narration, the ease, the lightness, the grace — above all, the perpetual wit, the play of delicate irony, which saves sentiment from being sentimental and erudition from being dull.

Dumas's style has been much abused, and in some ways deserves it. Mr. Saintsbury considers that the plays have 'but little value as literature properly so-called,' and that 'the style of the novels is not more remarkable as such than that of the dramas.' But how far more discerning and sympathetic is Stevenson's characterization of it: 'Light as a whipped trifle, strong as silk; wordy like a village tale; pat like a general's despatch; with every fault, yet never tedious; with no merit, yet inimitably right.' As for dialogue — that subtlest test of the novelist's genius — which neither Balzac, nor Flaubert, nor Zola could manage with flexibility or ease, Dumas may have used it to excess, but who has ever carried it to greater perfection? In M. Lemaître's excellent, if somewhat cynical, phrase, Dumas's dialogue has 'the wonderful quality of stringing out the narrative to the crack of doom and at the same time making it appear to move with headlong rapidity.' But let it string out, so it moves. And surely Dumas's conversations do move, as no others ever have.

In the hurry of modern reading, few people have time to get at Dumas in any but his best-known works. Yet to form a complete idea of his powers, one must take a much wider survey. All periods, all nations, all regions of the earth, came at one time or another under his pen. Of course this means an inevitable superficiality and inaccuracy. But one overlooks these defects, is hardly aware of them, in the ease, the spirit, the unfailing humanness of the narrative. Take a minor story like

'L'Isle de Feu,' dealing with the Dutch in Java and with the habits and superstitions of the natives, snake-charming, spirit-haunting, etc. Everywhere there is movement, life, character, the wit of the 'Impressions de Voyage,' the passion of 'La Reine Margot.' And if Dumas does not quite anticipate the seductive melancholy of Loti's tropics, he gives hints of it which are really wonderful for a man who had never been south of latitude thirty.

Perhaps, outside of the historical novels, we may select four very different books as most typical of Dumas's great variety of production. First, in 'Conscience l'Innocent,' we have a simple idyllic subject, recalling George Sand's country stories: peasant life, rural scenes, sweet pictures of Dumas's own village home at Villers-Cotterets, which he introduced into so many of his writings. Second, in the immense canvas of 'Salvator,' too little appreciated, we have a picture of contemporary conditions, the Paris of Sue and Hugo, treated with a vividness far beyond Sue and a dramatic power which Hugo never could command. Third, comes the incomplete 'Isaac Laquedem,' the vast Odyssey of the Wandering Jew, in which the author planned to develop epically the whole history of the world, though the censorship allowed him to get no further than the small Biblical portion of it. Few of Dumas's books illustrate better the really soaring sweep of his imagination, and not many have a larger share of his *esprit*. Lastly, there is 'Monte Cristo,' which, on the whole, remains, doubtless, the best example of what Dumas could do without history to support him. 'Pure melodrama,' some will say; in a sense, truly. Yet, as compared with the melodrama of, for instance, 'Armadale' and 'The Woman in White,' there is a certain largeness, a somber grandeur, about the vengeance of Dantès which goes almost far enough to lift the book out of the realm of melodrama, and into that of tragedy. And then there is the wit!

But it is on historical romance, whether in drama or fiction, that Dumas's popularity must chiefly rest. He himself felt it would be so, hoped it would be so; and his numerous references to the matter, if amusing, are also extremely interesting. He speaks of his series of historical novels as 'immense pictures we have undertaken to unroll before the eyes of our readers, in which, if our genius equalled our good will, we would introduce all classes of men from the beggar to the king, from Caliban to Ariel.' And again: 'Balzac has written a great work entitled "The Human Comedy." Our work, begun at the same time, may be entitled "The Drama of France."' He hopes that his labors will be profitable as well as amusing: 'We intentionally say "instruct" first, for amusement with us is only a mask for instruction. . . . Concerning the last five centuries and a half we have taught France more history than any historian.' And when some one gently insinuates that from a purely historical point of view his work cannot stand with the highest, he replies with his usual charming humor, 'It is the unreadable histories that make a stir; they are like dinners you can't digest; digestible dinners give you no cause to think about them on the next day.'

After all, humor apart, we must recognize the justice of Dumas's claim; and the enduring life and perpetual revival of the historical novel go far to support it. Mankind in general do love to hear about Henry IV, Richelieu, and the Stuarts, about Washington and Lincoln and Napoleon, and in hearing they do learn, even against their will. Pedants shake their heads. This birth-date is incorrect. That victory was not a victory at all. When Dr. Dryasdust has given the slow labor of a lifetime to disentangling fact from fiction, how wicked to mislead the ignorant by wantonly developing fiction out of fact! As if Dr. Dryasdust really knew fact from fiction! As if the higher spiritual facts were not altogether beyond his ken and his researches! As if any two pedants agreed! Take the central fact of history, the point from which everything of importance and interest emanates — human character, the human soul. What pedant can reach it, can analyse it with his finest microscope? Napoleon was born on such a day, died on such a day, this he did, that he did. But was he in any sense patriotic, an idealist, a lover of France? Was he a suspicious, jealous, lascivious tyrant? Was he sometimes one, sometimes the other? State documents and gossiping memoirs give no final answer to these questions, only hints and cloudy indications bearing upon them, from which the genius of the historian must sketch a figure for itself. Therefore, as many historians, so many Napoleons, and in the end my Napoleon, your Napoleon. If so, why not Alexandre Dumas's Napoleon, said Dumas, having perhaps as much faculty of imaginative divination as you or I, or even as several historians whom we will not mention.

In fact, Dumas has undoubtedly taught the history of France to thousands who would otherwise have had little concern with it. And his characters

live. Catherine de' Medici and her sons, Louis
XIV, Mazarin, the Duc de Richelieu, Marie An-
toinette — we know them as we know people whom
we meet every day: in one sense, perhaps not at all;
but in another sense, intimately. Great actions
call for a large background, which should be handled
with the wide sweep of the scene-painter, not with
the curious minuteness of the artist in miniatures.
The very abundance of these characters, the vastness of the canvas, help the reality, and in this
matter of amplitude Dumas and Scott show their
genius, and triumph over the petty concentration
of later imitators. Nor are the characters wholly or
mainly of Dumas's own invention less vivid than
those historical; for Dumas learned from Scott the
cardinal secret of historical romance, which Shakespeare did not grasp, that the action of the story
should turn, not on real personages, but on ficti-
tious heroes and heroines, whose fortunes can be
moulded freely for a dramatic purpose. Dumas
himself says somewhere that people complain of the
length of his novels, yet that the longest have been
the most popular and the most successful. It is so.
We can wander for days in the vast galleries of the
'Reine Margot' series, charmed with the gallantry
of La Mole, the vivacity of Coconnas, the bravado

of Bussy, above all, the inimitable wit and shrewdness of Chicot, who surely comes next to d'Artagnan among all Dumas's literary children. And
d'Artagnan — what a broad country he inhabits!
How lovely to lose one's self there in long winter
evenings, meeting at every turn a saucy face or a
gay gesture or a keen flash of sword that makes one
forget the passage of time. 'I never had a care
that a half-hour's reading would not dissipate,' said
Montesquieu. Fortunate man! How few of us resemble him! But if a half-hour's reading of anything would work such a miracle, surely a novel of
Dumas would do it.

As for the man himself, he happily created such
characters as d'Artagnan and Chicot because he re-
sembled them, and was in his own person as pictur-
esque a figure as any that talks passion in his plays,
or wit in the endless pages of his novels. I do not
know that he had ever read Milton's oracular saying that he who would be a great poet should make
his life a true poem; but, in any case, he pointed it
aptly by showing that the best way to write romantic novels is to make a romantic novel of your own
career. Born in 1802, in the most stirring period of
French history, one quarter African by blood, he
worked his way upward from bitter poverty and

insignificance to sudden glory and considerable wealth. Ambitious for political as well as literary success he took a more or less active part in the various commotions of the second quarter of the century, so that he was able to say of himself with some truth and immense satisfaction, 'I have touched the left hand of princes, the right hand of artists and literary celebrities, and have come in contact with all phases of life.'

A great traveler, a great hunter, he had innumerable adventures by flood and field. Quick in emotion and quicker in speech, he made friends everywhere and some enemies. Peculiarly sensitive to the charms and caresses of women, he had no end of love-affairs, all more or less discreditable. Thoughtless, careless, full of wit, full of laughter, he traveled the primrose way, plucking kisses like spring blossoms, wrapping his cloak more tightly round him when he ran into winter storms of envy, jealousy, and mocking. What wealth he had he squandered, what glory, he frittered away. And as he was born in a whirlwind of French triumph, so he died, in 1870, in a wilder whirlwind of French ruin and despair.

The man's life was, indeed, a novel; and in writing his 'Memoirs' he dressed it out as such, height-ening, coloring, enriching the golden web of memory, as only he knew how to do; so that I am almost ready to call these same memoirs the best of his works, even with 'Les Trois Mousquetaires' and 'La Tour de Nesle' in fresh remembrance. Such variety and vivacity of anecdote, such vivid, shifting portraiture of characters, such quick reality of incident, such wit always. But the best of it, unquestionably, is not Talma, nor Dorval, nor Hugo, nor the Duke of Orleans, but just Alexandre Dumas. It is said that once, when a friend asked him how he had enjoyed a party, Dumas replied, 'I should have been horribly bored, if it hadn't been for myself.' Readers of the 'Memoirs' will easily understand how other society might have seemed dull in comparison.

From all the tangled mass of anecdote and laughter let us try to gather one or two definite lines of portraiture for the better understanding of this singular personage, 'one of the forces of nature,' as Michelet called him in a phrase which Dumas loved to repeat.

And to begin with the beginning. Did the creator of Buridan and Chicot have a religion, did he trouble himself with abstract ideas? You smile; and certainly he did not trouble his readers very

much with these things. Yet in his own opinion he
was a thinker, and a rather deep one. Read, in the
preface to 'Caligula,' how the public received with
awe 'this rushing torrent of thought, which appeared to it perhaps new and daring, but solemn
and chaste; and then withdrew, with bowed head,
like a man who has at last found the solution of a
problem which has vexed him during many sleep-
less nights.'

In his turbulent youth the author of 'Antony'
was a disbeliever, as became a brother of Byron and
Musset; 'there are moments when I would give thee
up my soul, if I believed I had one.' But in later
years he settled down to the soberer view which appears in the dedication of 'La Conscience' to Hugo:
'in testimony of a friendship which has survived
exile and will, I hope, survive death. I believe in
the immortality of the soul.' And again and again
he testified to the power of his early religious training, which 'left upon all my beliefs, upon all my
opinions, so profound an impression that even to-
day I cannot enter a church without taking the
holy water, cannot pass a crucifix without making
the sign of the cross.' Nor do these emotions spring
from mere religiosity, but from an astonishingly,
not to say crudely, definite form of belief: 'I know

not what my merit has been, whether in this world or in the other worlds I may have inhabited before; but God has shown me especial favors and in all the critical situations in which I have found myself, he has come visibly to my assistance. Therefore, O God, I confess thy name openly and humbly before all skeptics and before all believers.' What revivalist of to-day could speak with more fervor? If only one did not suspect a bit of the irony that shows more clearly in the conversation with his old teacher, whose prayers Dumas had requested. 'My prayers?' said the abbé. 'You don't believe in them.' — 'No, I don't always believe in them. That is very true; but don't worry: when I need them I will believe in them.' On the strength of that remark we might almost call Dumas the inventor of Pragmatism before Professor James.

And the irony is rooted in a truth of character. Dumas was a man of this world. He might dream of the other at odd moments, in vague curiosity; but by temperament he was a frank pagan, an eater, a laugher, a lover, a fighter, gorgeously in words, not wholly ineffectively in deeds, even after we have made the necessary discount from his own version of his exploits. He had inherited something of his father's magnificent physique and something of his father's courage. When he tells us that 'since I arrived at manhood, whenever danger has presented itself, by night or by day, I have always walked straight up to danger,' we believe him — with the discount aforesaid; and we believe him all the more, because like every brave man, he does not hesitate to confess fear. 'It was the first time I had heard the noise of grapeshot, and I say frankly that I will not believe any one who tells me that he heard that noise for the first time without perturbation.'

In truth, the religion, the courage, the fear — all, and everything else in the man, were a matter of impulse, of immediate emotion. He was quite aware of this himself. When he proposed his Vendée mission to Lafayette, the latter said to him, 'Have you reflected on what this means?' — 'As much as I am capable of reflecting about anything: I am a man of instinct, not of reflection.' The extraordinary vanity of which he was justly accused, of which he accuses himself — 'everybody knows the vain side of my character' — was only one phase of this natural impulsiveness. He spoke out what others think — and keep to themselves. Mr. Davidson has admirably noted that in Dumas's case vanity was perfectly compatible with humility.

He had no absurdly exaggerated idea of his own powers. But he liked to talk about himself, to be conspicuous, to be the central figure on every stage. The African blood, of which he was not ashamed — 'I am a mulatto,' he says repeatedly — told in him; the negro childlikeness. He was a child always, above all childlike in this matter of vanity. Readers of 'Tom Sawyer' will remember that that delightful youth, on hearing the beatific vision of Isaiah, which pictures such a varied menagerie dwelling in harmony, with a little child to lead them, had one absorbing wish: that he might be that child. Dumas was precisely like Tom Sawyer; witness this delightful prayer of his youth: 'Make me great and glorious, O Lord, that I may come nearer unto thee. And the more glorious thou makest me, the more humbly will I confess thy name, thy majesty, thy splendor.'

The same childlike temper, the fresh, animal instincts of a great boy, explain, if they do not excuse, the disorders of Dumas's life.

In this connection it is hardly necessary to do more than to point out his hopeless aberration from all Anglo-Saxon standards of propriety and decency. It would be easy to lash such aberration, but it is perhaps better to consider it in connection with the man's character as a whole, and to remember that his life was as far as possible from being a generally idle or dissipated one. He never smoked, cherishing, in fact, a grudge against tobacco, which he regarded as an enemy to true sociability. He was moderate in eating and drinking. Above all, he was an enormous worker. No man essentially vicious, no man who had not a large fund of temperance and self-control, could have produced a tithe of Dumas's legacy to posterity. But what is most interesting of all in this matter of morals is Dumas's entire satisfaction with himself. I doubt if any other human being would deliberately have ventured on a statement so remarkable as the following: 'When the hand of the Lord closes the two horizons of my life, letting fall the veil of his love between the nothingness that precedes and the nothingness that follows the life of man, he may examine the intermediate space with his most rigorous scrutiny, he will not find there one single evil thought or one action for which I feel that I should reproach myself.' Comment on this would only dim its splendor. Yet people say that the 'Memoirs' of Dumas lack interest as human documents! He was an atrocious hypocrite, then, you think? Not the least in the world. Simply a child, always a child.

A child in money matters also. No one could accuse him of deliberate financial dishonesty; but to beg and borrow and never to pay was the normal condition of things. To promise right and left when cash was needed, then to find one's self entirely unable to fulfil one's promises — still childlike. Only, persons of that childlike temper, who have not genius, are apt to end badly. And then, after all, to write in cold blood that one has never had a single action to reproach one's self with! I trust the reader appreciates that passage as I do.

And if the child lacked a sense of money property, how should he be likely to have a sense of property in literature? Shakespeare, Schiller, dozens of others, had had ideas which were useful. Why not use them? A few persons had previously written on the history of France. Distinguished historical characters had left memoirs describing their own achievements. It would have been almost disrespectful to neglect the valuable material thus afforded. Let us quote the histories and borrow from the memoirs. As for mentioning any little indebtedness, life is not long enough for that. We make bold to think that what we invent is quite as good as what we take from others. So it is — far better. A careful comparison of 'Les Trois Mous-

quetaires' with the original d'Artagnan 'Memoirs'
increases rather than diminishes one's admiration
for the author of the novel.

But it will be said, even after borrowing his material, Dumas could not write this same novel without the assistance of a certain Maquet. Again the
same childlike looseness in the sense of property.
Could a genius be expected to write three hundred [1]
volumes without helpers for the rough work? He
must have hodmen to fetch bricks and mortar. And
perhaps the builder, hurried and overdriven, may
set the hodmen to lay a bit of wall here and there,
may come to leave altogether too much to hodmen
so that the work suffers for it. What matter? Had
ever any Maquet or Gaillardet or Meurice, writing
by himself, the Dumas touch? As Mr. Lang justly
points out, no collaborator has been suggested for
the 'Memoirs' and I have already said that the
'Memoirs' belong, in many respects, to Dumas's
best, most characteristic work.

Then, a child is as ready to give as to take. So
was Dumas. In money matters it goes without saying. He was always ready to give, to give to every-

[1] Perhaps it would be well to explain the different numerical esti-
mates of Dumas's works. As now published in the Lévy collection
they fill about three hundred volumes, but in their original form they
ran to twelve hundred, more or less.

body everything he had, and even everything he had not and some one else had. 'Nature had already put in my heart,' he says of his childhood, 'that fountain of general kindliness through which flows away and will flow away, everything I had, everything I have, and everything I ever shall have.' But it was not only money, it was time and thought, labor and many steps. This same fountain of general kindliness was always at the service even of strangers. For instance, Dumas himself tells us that, happening once to be in a seaport town, he found a young couple just sailing for the islands and very desolate. He set himself to cheer them up, and his efforts were so well received that he could not find it in his heart to leave them, though pressing business called him away. He went on board ship with them, and only returned on the pilot boat, in the midst of a gale and at the peril of his life, so says the story. Even in the matter of literary collaboration, Mr. Davidson justly points out that Dumas gave as well as took, and that the list of his debtors is longer than that of his creditors.

And in the highest generosity, that of sympathy and appreciation for fellow workers, the absence of envy and meanness in rivalry, Dumas is nobly abundant. He tells us so himself, not having the habit of concealing his virtues: 'Having arrived at the summit which every man finds in the middle of life's journey, I ask nothing, I desire nothing, I envy nothing, I have many friendships and not one single hatred.' More reliable evidence lies in the general tone of enthusiasm and admiration with which he speaks of all his contemporaries. Musset avoided him, Balzac insulted him; yet he refers to both with hearty praise very different from the damning commendations of the envious Sainte-Beuve. Lamartine and Hugo he eulogizes with lavish freedom, not only in the often-quoted remark, 'Hugo is a thinker, Lamartine a dreamer, and I am a popularizer' — a remark more generous than discriminating — but in innumerable passages which leave no possible doubt of his humility and sincerity. 'Style was what I lacked above everything else. If you had asked me for ten years of my life, promising in exchange that one day I should attain the expression of Hugo's 'Marion Delorme,' I should not have hesitated, I should have given them instantly.'

These things make Dumas attractive, lovable even, as few French writers are lovable. With all his faults he has something of the personal charm of Scott. Only something, however; for Scott, no whit less generous, less kindly, had the sanity, the stability, the moral character, why avoid the word? which Dumas had not. And in comparing their works — a comparison which suggests itself almost inevitably; 'Scott, the grandfather of us all,' said Dumas himself — this difference of morals strikes us even more than the important differences of style and handling of character. It is the immortal merit of Scott that he wrote novels of love and adventure as manly, as virile, as heart can wish, yet absolutely pure.

Now, Dumas has the grave disadvantage of not knowing what morals — sexual morals — are. Listen to him: 'Of the six hundred volumes (1848) that I have written, there are not four which the hand of the most scrupulous mother need conceal from her daughter.' The reader who knows Dumas only in 'Les Trois Mousquetaires' will wonder by what fortunate chance he has happened on two volumes out of those 'not four.' But he may reassure himself. There are others of the six hundred which, to use the modern French perversion, more effective untranslated, the daughter will not recommend to her mother. The truth is, Dumas's innocence is worse than, say, Maupassant's sophistication. To the author of 'La Reine Margot' love, so called, is all, the excuse, the justification, for everything. Marriage — *ça n'existe pas;* Dumas knew all about it. He was married himself for a few months — at the king's urgent suggestion. Then he recommended the lady to the ambassador at Florence with a most polite note, and she disappeared from his too flowery career. Therefore, Dumas begins his love-stories where Scott's end, and the delicate refinement, the pure womanly freedom of Jeannie Deans and Diana Vernon, is missing in the Frenchman's young ladies, who all either wish to be in a nunnery or ought to be.

The comparison with Scott suggests another with a greater than Scott; and like Scott, Dumas did not object to being compared with Shakespeare, who, by the way, has never been more nobly praised in a brief sentence than in Dumas's saying that 'he was the greatest of all creators after God.' There are striking resemblances between the two writers. Shakespeare began in poverty, lived among theatrical people, made a fortune by the theater. Only, being a thrifty English *bourgeois,* he put the fortune into his own pocket instead of into others'. Shakespeare made a continuous show of English history and bade the world attend it. Shakespeare begged, borrowed, and stole from dead and living, so that his contemporaries spoke of his

'Tiger's heart wrapped in a player's hide.'

Doubtless Maquet and Gaillardet would have been willing to apply the phrase to their celebrated collaborator. Thus far the comparison works well enough. But Shakespeare had a style which was beyond even that of 'Marion Delorme.' And then, Shakespeare felt and thought as a man, not as a child; his brain and his heart carried the weight of the world.

What will be the future of Dumas? Will his work pass, as other novels of romantic adventure have passed? Three hundred years ago idle women — and men — read 'Amadis de Gaul' and the like, with passion. Says the waiting-woman in Massinger's 'Guardian':

'In all the books of *Amadis de Gaul*
The *Palmerins* and that true Spanish story,
The Mirror of Knighthood, which I have read often,
Read feelingly, nay, more, I do believe in't,
My lady has no parallel.'

Where are *Amadis* and the *Palmerins* now? Two hundred years ago the same persons read with the same passion the novels of Scudéry and La Calprenède. 'At noon home,' says Mr. Pepys, 'where I find my wife troubled still at my checking her last night in the coach in her long stories out of 'Grand Cyrus,' which she would tell, though nothing to the purpose, nor in any good manner.' And hear Madame de Sévigné on 'Cléopatre': 'The style of La Calprenède is abominable in a thousand places: long sentences in the full-blown, romantic fashion, ill-chosen words — I am perfectly aware of it. Yet it holds me like glue. The beauty of the sentiments, the violent passions, the great scale on which everything takes place and the miraculous success of the hero's redoubtable sword — it carries me away, as if I were a young girl.' *Le succès miraculeux de leur redoutable épée;* if one tried a thousand times, could one express more precisely and concisely one's feelings about 'Les Trois Mousquetaires'? Yet 'Grand Cyrus' is dead, and 'Cléopatre' utterly forgotten. No bright-eyed girl asks for them in any circulating library any more.

Shall d'Artagnan, 'dear d'Artagnan,' as Stevenson justly calls him — 'I do not say that there is no character so well drawn in Shakespeare; I do say that there is none I love so wholly' — d'Artagnan, whose *redoutable épée* makes such delightful havoc among the nameless *canaille*, whose more redoubtable wit sets kings and queens and dukes and cardi-

nals at odds and brings them to peace again —
shall d'Artagnan, too, die and be forgotten? The
thought is enough to make one close 'Le Vicomte
de Bragelonne' in the middle and fall a-dreaming
on the flight of time and the changes of the world.
And one says to one's self that one would like to
live two or three centuries for many reasons, but
not least, to read stories so absorbing that they
will make one indifferent to the adventures of
d'Artagnan.

1908

VIII
A FRENCH LAMB

VIII

A FRENCH LAMB

W<small>HY</small> is it that the few brief notes which accompany Lamb's selections from the old English dramatic poets live in the memory of all who love literature? It is because Lamb did not attempt to formulate principles or grade perfections, or lay down everlasting rules for the guidance of poets, past and future. He was all alive himself, keenly sensitive to human joy and human passion, and he went unerringly to every trace of these things in the forgotten beauty before him, sometimes lending it his own life, but making it live always. 'It is difficult to get rid of a woman at the end of a tragedy. Men may fight and die. A woman must either take poison, which is a nasty trick, or go mad, which is not fit to be shown — or retire, which is poor; only retiring is most reputable.' This is not quite the manner of Aristotle or Lessing; but it makes us think, it makes us feel, and if it makes us smile also, where is the harm?

I wish that every one who loves Lamb might know the ten volumes of M. Jules Lemaître's 'Impressions de Théâtre.' Not that M. Lemaître's

temperament or view of life resembles Lamb's very
closely. But there is the same treatment of the
drama as a live thing, the same keen, petulant interest in all phases of humanity, often displaying
itself in the discussion of a trifling subject or a
minor personage. Lamb will make the most delicate turn of observation apropos of a dead play of
Brome or Shirley. So M. Lemaître writes of a hissed
piece by some forgotten author, and wit and grace
and sympathetic insight make his criticism of far
greater charm and permanent value than the thing
criticized.

Nothing will show this better than a comparison
of M. Lemaître's work with the collected volumes
of articles by Sarcey, 'Quarante Ans de Théâtre.'
Sarcey's criticism is of very great value and interest.
It not only bears on the French drama of his own
day, but is full of fruitful lessons for the dramatist
of all time. Sarcey, however, is often accused of
being conventional, of thinking only of the technical aspects of theatrical workmanship, of caring
more about how a play was made than about the
matter of it. It is, at any rate, true that he was
keenly alive to popular success. 'Plays were written
to please the public,' he argued, 'and they must
please. Let us find out, if possible, why some please

and some do not.' In making this curious investigation he, perhaps, did not sufficiently consider that there are publics and publics, perhaps identified himself a little too much with the average man, without reflecting that work aimed at the average man is likely to be average work. With his frank gayety, his good nature, his large common sense, he was perhaps something of an average man himself.

When we turn to 'Impressions de Théâtre,' we are in a totally different atmosphere. The subjects are the same, but the method is not. The perishable quality, the mere temporary fortune of a play, is of minor importance. Instantly the critic lifts it out of such trivial relations and discusses its failure or success in achieving human truth, not, however, with a cumbrous apparatus of philosophical theory, but with a sympathetic desire to get at the essence of things, as unpretentious as it is sincere. Nothing could be more charming than M. Lemaître's attitude toward Sarcey. The younger critic appreciates perfectly the elder's wide experience, his sane, large receptivity, his jovial common sense. Half a dozen times his talks on the older dramatists are reported by his brilliant rival with a delicate current of irony which must have delighted Sarcey more than any one else. In discussing the 'Antigone' of Sophocles, M. Lemaître summarizes the article Sarcey would have written on the tragedy had it been the work of a young contemporary. 'The play swarms with moral improbabilities . . . but in the eyes of these young literary enthusiasts the most established principles are mere old-fogeyism. There is a certain grandeur in the thing, I confess, and style. But it is not drama.'

In M. Lemaître's work, then, we find dramatic criticism hardly more than an excuse for the finest and most delicate observation and study of human nature. The French term 'moralist' so different from the English, meaning not a preacher, but a student, not a reformer, but a psychologist, applies to him as much as to Joubert or La Bruyère. Only, whereas those celebrated authors put their wisdom into detached, concentrated bits, not always comfortably readable, his is diffused in a continuous current flowing easily along a definite line and holding the attention almost as steadily as narrative or drama. For instance, he is writing about Meilhac and Halévy's 'Réveillon.' The second act is a supper scene. He remarks that it is exceptional in being amusing, since almost all such scenes upon the stage are apt to be unnatural and dull. Then, in looking for the reason of this, he analyzes, with cunning insight, the psychology of a supper or dinner party — oh, not by laboratory methods or the metric system, but with sympathy and dramatic gift that make you feel as if you were there yourself — and shows that the authors, by an instinctive art, have contrived to put just this natural process on the stage. Or, in a more serious vein — though, as with Lamb, the serious and the gay with M. Lemaître go always hand in hand — take this fine analysis with which the critic — again in connection with Meilhac and Halévy — discusses the possibilities of profound truth underneath the lightest farce. 'I hesitate to assert that there is depth in this comedy. MM. Meilhac and Halévy have so much wit that perhaps they have enough to laugh at me, if I assert it, and I assure you a man must be witty indeed to laugh at those who accuse him of profundity. . . . But don't you think that taken by their serious side and brought down to human proportions, the personage of Blue Beard, as he sees himself, and that of Boulotte ending (oh, dark places of the heart) by loving Blue Beard, might become haughty and mysterious tragic figures so rich in substance that it would be possible to reason and debate about them as much at length as one may about Hamlet?' As the converse of this, one should read also everything that M. Lemaître writes about Ibsen; for, mingled with a profound admiration for the great Norwegian, there is also an irony as keen as it is gentle, probing the solemn emptiness which clouds and deadens much of his work.

This irony, this delightful blend of wit with tenderness, much like Lamb's, though less riotous, less whimsical, less broadly frolicsome, than Lamb's, appears on every page of M. Lemaître's writing and is one of its greatest charms. It is never intrusive, never inappropriate; you never feel — I never feel — that it in any way degrades great things; but it lends grace to difficult matters and charm to dull ones. It is like the indefinable witchery of a Frenchwoman's talk which makes you glad to listen to her even when she speaks of the indifferent or commonplace. This quality, which comes often nearer to English humor than to the true Voltairean wit, has appeared in what I have so far quoted and will in what I quote further; but over and over again in M. Lemaître's work it charms us purely for itself. Take, for instance, this petulant protest against modern nature worship. (Lamb, you remember, rebelled in the same way against the mute prostrations of his Lake friends:) 'For my part if anybody says to me, "Don't you adore the whispering of poplars in dark midnight?" I answer, "Do you?" And if he adds, "Don't you love the song of the linnet, the lark's cry, and the brook's murmur?" I reply: "Of course, of course. But, unfortunately, I don't hear such things often. And then — you can't live on them. And don't think badly of me — but really I know other pleasures that are a little keener than those."' Another delightful example of M. Lemaître's sense of comedy — this time surely humorous, if ever anything was — is his account of the meeting between Renan and the concert-hall singer, Victorine Demay: 'The author of the "Life of Jesus," with his well known politeness and charming good nature, came up to the singer and said to her, "Madame, I rarely visit concert-halls, but I shall enjoy listening to you, for I have heard your name often." Demay, quite overcome and wishing to be as amiable as possible, made this reply, surely grand in its simplicity, "I also know you very well, indeed." Isn't that admirable when one imagines to one's self what Demay could know of M. Renan and what idea she could possibly have of him?'

Without doubt the freedom and the richness of

M. Lemaître's criticism are closely connected with
his theory of what criticism should be, and here
again, though Lamb might not have agreed with
him in the abstract, they are quite at one in their
practice. The French love names, and M. Lemaître frequently proclaims himself an impressionist. Perhaps, with M. Anatole France, he is —
or was at the time of writing the 'Impressions' —
the leading representative of that school. But names
are cold and limiting, easily outgrown and too subject to definition by the ignorant. Probably M.
Lemaître would always have admitted that certain
principles lie at the bottom of all art judgment.
Only he would have urged that these principles are
too general to go far and are difficult of practical
application. He would have heartily agreed with
Sterne that 'of all the cants that are canted in this
canting world, the cant of hypocrisy may be the
worst, but surely the cant of criticism is the most
tormenting.' To him the charm of art is its freedom, its variety. In practical action we must be
hampered and trammelled by standards and conventions. Let us at least keep the art world as clear
as possible from the formula of the professor and the
tape-measure of the connoisseur. Let us recognize
that every age has its right and every tempera-

ment its privilege, not insist too harshly on straining new thought into old moulds, above all, not fight, with bookish ingenuity, for old moulds because they are ours and we are used to them. The secret of life is growth, change. 'Behold! I make all things new.' To be sure, the new is rooted in the old and established upon it. We must know the past and love it. But we must be ready for every fresh revelation, open-minded, liberal, eager to adapt ourselves to new forms and new conditions, apt to reject what is dead when it is dead. Only so can we be sure of being fruitfully alive. The expression of these principles is everywhere to be found in M. Lemaître's work, in the earlier and, as I think, inferior, volumes of 'Les Contemporains,' more crude and combative, in the 'Impressions de Théâtre' more subtle, more persuasive, more in-sinuating: 'For my part I accept everything; I enjoy everything in its time, turn and turn about or even all at once: reality that is grotesque and low, reality that is ennobled by artistic treatment, classical idealism, romanticism, naturalism. Ra-cine as well as Balzac, George Sand as well as Émile Zola, Bourget as well as Maupassant.... I like everything, because everything is true, even dreams. Whatever may be the aspect of things that presents itself to the artist, I will make it mine, provided the form of it is instinct with beauty.'

This impressionist attitude of criticism is often objected to as being personal and so impertinent. You have nothing to give us but your own experiences, your own sensations: what do we care for those? It seems to me that in reality the opposite dogmatic fashion of criticizing is the impertinent one. 'This is beautiful by all the eternal laws and standards. I say so. You must accept it whether you like it or not.' I find it hard to relish that, even when it comes from Ruskin or Arnold. The dogmatism, the sharp decisions, of a Brunetière are well enough when you agree with them. When you do not, they savor of egotism to a considerable degree. There are no sharp decisions in M. Lemaître. He would say: 'I do not ask you to follow me. I do not wish you to follow me. Certain things have moved me, touched me, helped me, delighted me. I will tell you of my delight, so far as I can, of the nature of it. It may be that the same delight will come to you also, or it may not. The result will be curious in either case.'

And I do not find the least touch of undue egotism in any detail of personal experience by which the critic seeks to convey and make clear to me this æsthetic rapture of his own. For I know that he is a man, as I am, that much of his experience is my experience, and that what is not mine is that of millions of others and will throw light on mine by the very difference. He tells me that he is not a Christian, but that he loves Christianity; and that at once explains his attitude toward many plays and many dramatic characters. He tells me of his boyhood reveries and passions, and I understand his love of Musset. He tells me that he did not read Dumas till he was a grown man, and I understand why 'Monte Cristo' bores him. Some persons may think it an odd thing for an author to write the criticisms of his own plays. It is perfectly consistent with M. Lemaître's theory, and in practice I find it not only charming, but most instructive as regards the author and the plays and some interesting questions of dramatic art in general. M. Lemaître himself has discussed this matter of introducing the critic's personality, and the following passage seems to me as reasonable as it is suggestive: 'A critic has the right to speak of himself, in so far as he is a critic and in his relation to the things he is called upon to criticize. It is even his duty, whenever he appreciates keenly what

there is of the relative and the merely temporary
in the judgments he formulates; whenever his personal confidences may help his readers to complete
or to rectify his judgments; in brief, whenever he is
not very sure of himself and feels himself to be
particularly fallible. I would even say that in doing
this he shows modesty, not assurance or presump-
tion. There is much more pride in the criticism
which is impersonal, because that does not avow
its fragility.'

Thus, like Lamb, M. Lemaître tells us a great
deal about himself and herein lies much of his
charm. He tells us frequently that he is French;
but that was hardly necessary, it is so obvious. He
is as French as Lamb is English. He is French in
his ignorance — ignorance of other countries and
their ways. 'As I know very little of foreign countries and their literature, I am not surprised at
anything that comes from them.' What English
or German critic would even set up to be a critic
after such a confession as that? But M. Lemaître
is French not only in his ignorance; he is so in his
deplorable contentment to be ignorant. He thinks
his country can afford to neglect the work of others
because she is so fruitful in masterpieces of her
own.

And his taste is as thoroughly French as his equipment. I confess that I myself owe to him large revelations of the grace, the perfection, the moral insight, more than that, the high tragic power of Racine. But as a French critic he perceives depth and beauty in many portions of Racine's work where they are hidden from me. Conversely his frankness, not to say irreverence, in dealing with Shakespeare is to me refreshing as a sea breeze. I so often feel about our English idol what M. Lemaître himself says in regard to Corneille: 'When one tries to receive from these venerable authors impressions as direct and sincere as if one read them for the first time, one falls almost inevitably from superstition into irreverence. Thus there are books as to which I have no opinion whatever and never shall have. I am, as it were, condemned never to know them because I know them too well.' Therefore, when I read that the last two acts of 'Hamlet' are 'extremely tedious,' that 'the conduct of Claudius is absurd, the queen null and absolutely passive, the gravedigger's scene in no way useful to the action, a dismal sort of comedy which with time has become horribly commonplace,' and that 'the scene of Ophelia's madness reminds you of a chromo,' while I may not agree, I am not wholly offended. Though when the critic proceeds to reaffirm Voltaire's celebrated dictum about 'the drunken savage,' I cannot but remember that I too 'speak the tongue which Shakespeare spake' and which M. Lemaître apparently has some difficulty in even reading.

French in morals also is M. Lemaître. Oh, not to any wild excess, but French. The delightful article on Renan's 'Abbesse de Jouarre,' for example, contains sound common sense about matters of sex. Any English critic would regard its substance as conservative and practical. But no English critic would dare to express himself on the subject with such airy frivolity. Again, the paper on Mary Magdalen is intended as a real, a sincere protest of reverence against the degradation of sacred things, but I should not venture to translate or even to paraphrase the vivid sparkles of Gallic wit which give it all its point and sting. These French employ such odd weapons in the service of morality that really — Yet no one can question the honesty of M. Lemaître's intentions or his profound sympathy with what is pure, austere, and noble in love matters as in other things. Like a certain far more celebrated personage whose

sympathies were sometimes stronger than his con-
victions, he

> 'Saw
> Virtue in her shape how lovely, saw and pined
> His loss.'

In morals non-sexual M. Lemaître's sensitive-
ness is even more keen, more delicate, more finely
tempered. Not that he is anything of a preacher
or assails vice with the stormy severity of a Ruskin
or a Carlyle. Far from it. Irony is his weapon,
an irony so tolerant, so sympathetic, that a hasty
reader might not even feel its force. He lashes no
wrong-doer: he knows too well himself the vast
ease of human wrong-doing. Yet on every page
you feel his resentment and protest against the
hard, eager materialism of modern life, his ardent
desire that somehow, somewhere, love might be
substituted for hate, and pity for selfishness. Only
he feels pity, not hatred, for the selfish and believes that they, after all, are the ones who suffer
most for their own sins.

This note of pity is one of the most marked
things about M. Lemaître's work, and it is the
union of pity and the sense of human misery with
his constant light and graceful humor which gives
everything he writes its singular charm. If the

consciousness of suffering may, perhaps, be called morbid, as in Zola, it is at least to be remarked that, as in Zola, it is absolutely impersonal. One never gets that impression of a tedious whine over the writer's own annoyances which is so characteristic of Carlyle and Thackeray. M. Lemaître's pity is for humanity at large, for the blind agony of millions struggling with adverse fate. He would say with Bosola:

'In what a shadow or deep pit of darkness
   Doth womanish and fearful mankind live.'

Especially is M. Lemaître's pity given to the poor and lowly. Here again he is French, and the conservative Anglo-Saxon will, perhaps, find him too lenient to something like anarchism, too ready to impute to society and its present organization evils which are inherent in the nature of man in any society. 'Our industrial civilization, which after all, is a benefit to only the small minority and imposes on such a number of men a life which is actually unhuman. . . . There are in Paris thousands of women who, after they have done their household work, make garments ten hours a day to earn eight or ten cents. And what food! And what lodging! And what a life! And even these are not the most unfortunate.' Much as one may pity the laborer, one may also feel that the *Bourgeois*, the middle class (especially when one belongs to it one's self) does not quite deserve all M. Lemaître's condemnation. 'The true enemy of Jesus in all countries, in all ages has been the *bourgeois.*' Perhaps Jesus died even for the bourgeois — a little. Yet so simple, so genuine, so honest is M. Lemaître's sympathy that these brief bursts of rhetoric do not in any way detract from it. He himself is eager to disclaim the attitude of agitator or apostle, to prick the bubble of high-sounding phrases which are not built on action. 'It is disloyal and disgraceful to parade ideas which, if one were really possessed by them, would compel one to sacrifice and renunciation and acts of virtue of which one knows one's self to be quite incapable. But pity is beautiful, even indignant pity, if only it is humble, and if a little of the indignation is turned against ourselves. For then good works may follow, or at least a small beginning of good works and the effort for them.' So in M. Lemaître's criticism, where one would least expect it, in the discussion of a farce of Labiche or of a dance-hall ballad, you may find touches of the deepest, tenderest human feeling, just as you find them in Lamb when he speaks of an old dead tragedy or of an actor who has been forgotten a hundred years.

And as Lamb, speaking of a friend whose children were to be brought up in their mother's Catholic faith, remarks 'I am resolved that my children shall be brought up in their father's religion — if they can find out what it is,' so M. Lemaître would doubtless bid us seek for his religion and would earnestly and devoutly join us in the search. I am not now speaking of later phases of M. Lemaître's career, as to which my information is somewhat conflicting. The writer of the 'Impressions de Théâtre' is seeking, always seeking. It is to be noted how totally different this later nineteenth-century skepticism is from that of Voltaire. It has nothing of Voltaire's joyous certainty of denial, nothing of his militant confidence in a critical power to build up as well as to overthrow. The unbelievers of a later time, like Renan, France, Lemaître, have no desire to overthrow anything. The beliefs of the old age are too remote from them to be worthy of attack, too full of sweetness and ancient reverence and manifold blessing to humanity to be treated with disdain. So far M. France and M. Lemaître, whose names are so often coupled, pull together. But only so far. M. France is a spiritual Epicurean perfectly content to be nothing further. All phases of religious emotion are to him a delightful study, like the phases of other emotion, especially amorous. He analyzes them, he feels them, he loves them, and goes on his way. M. Lemaître is no Epicurean, though his spiritual delight is perhaps quite as keen as that of M. France. The pity of the world, its agony will not let him rest. Keen wit, buoyant gayety, broad sympathy with every form of beauty, do not hide or hush for him the eternal question. Perhaps they make it sting more sharply. He is too honest to take unsatisfactory answers. He is too earnest to rest wholly satisfied with none. And it is this constant, restless sense of the deeper things of life, combined with human insight and with the most varied resource of literary charm, that make the 'Impressions de Théâtre' far more than a mere parasitical comment on the ephemeral productions of the Paris stage, a collection of essays of choice and permanent value which ought to be read and enjoyed more and more as time goes on, if the overwhelming growth of literature leaves any man or woman time to read at all.

1909

IX
A GREAT ENGLISH PORTRAIT-PAINTER

IX

A GREAT ENGLISH PORTRAIT-PAINTER

ENGLAND has no great portrait-painter of the Renaissance to put beside those of Italy, of the Low Countries, and of Spain. If her brave men and fair women of the first part of the seventeenth century still live on canvas, it is mainly thanks to a foreign artist who found early that the English could pay, though they could not paint. They could also use the pen, if not the brush. Neither Sir Joshua nor Gainsborough later, not even Vandyke or Velasquez or Titian, could have painted English gentlemen more grandly or more imperishably than did Edward Hyde, Earl of Clarendon.

He has painted himself at full length, at very great length, with a power and an insight not uncomparable to the best in the Uffizi chamber of self-portraiture. Side by side with his great 'History' runs the slighter current of his own 'Life,' slighter, but clearer, gayer, more vivid, with less ample curve, less solid majesty, as a plain prose outline by a finished poem.

He was a man who mingled early with great

people and great things and liked to look upward; for he 'never knew one man, of what condition soever, arrive to any degree of reputation in the world who made choice of or delighted in the company or conversation of those who were inferior or in their parts not much superior to himself.' It was thus that he sought the society of Selden, of Cowley, of Carew, of Ben Jonson, who knew the human heart and perhaps taught his young friend some of its secrets. Of Selden, Hyde says, simply (writing as usual in the third person), 'He always thought himself best when he was with him.'

Then there came days of trouble in England, and Hyde was in the thick of it, so that no man ever lived who had more chance of seeing good sides of human nature, bad sides, all sides, than he. He not only saw, but acted with hand and brain. He loved freedom, but he also loved old, sacred things, and stood for the Crown, if not always for the King. His masters made him Lord Chancellor, and listened to his advice, and sometimes heeded it, and sometimes not, and perhaps might not have profited even if they had.

Then came ruin and despair and exile. And Hyde was often wise and always faithful. With the Restoration he grew very great and was honest at

heart and strove against the overwhelming stream
of corruption about him perhaps as effectually as
one man could. 'Had it not been for the firmness
of the Earl of Clarendon the liberties of the nation
had been delivered up,' says the blunt Burnet.
And Pepys: 'I am mad in love with my Lord Chancellor, for he do comprehend and speak out well and
with the greatest easiness and authority that ever
I saw man in my life. . . . He spoke indeed excellent well; . . . his manner and freedom of doing it
as if he played with it, and was informing only all
the rest of the company, was mighty pretty.'

Here we begin to detect the weaknesses, as, indeed, they may be detected in the man's own account of himself. He was haughty and unapproach-
able, 'a man not to be advised, thinking himself too
high to be counseled,' says Pepys again. Worse
still, damnably worse, to Charles the Second's
thinking, he was tedious. Says Burnet: 'He was
also all that while giving the King many wise and
good advices, but he did it too much with the air of
a governor or a lawyer.' What the King felt about
it Clarendon himself lets us see, involuntarily,
when he writes of the Stuarts in general: 'They did
not love the conversation of men of many more
years than themselves, and thought age not only

troublesome but impertinent.' And I say to my-self Polonius, oh, Polonius, for all the world! Polonius was wise and shrewd and really full of good counsel. But he was tedious. And that other great painter, Saint-Simon, also played a weary Polonius to the mad Duke of Orleans.

So the King's patience gave out at last. That of others had given out long before. The Chancellor made a good fight, recovering himself again and again when no recovery seemed possible. But his enemies were too many for him, and succeeded in driving him once more into exile, from which he never returned. He bore himself bravely, which was well. And prided himself on it, which was per-haps less well. He himself says: 'The truth is the Chancellor was guilty of that himself which he had used to accuse Archbishop Laud of, that he was too proud of a good conscience.' Nevertheless, he con-fesses with charming frankness the very one of his faults which was most treasured against him, his love of grandeur, display, extravagance; and ad-mits the folly of his huge new mansion, which over-shadowed the King's: 'He could not reflect upon any one thing he had done of which he was so much ashamed as he was of the vast expense he had made in the building of his house.' He 'could not find any house to live in except he built one himself (to which he was naturally too much inclined).' And in exile 'he remained still so much infected with the delight he had enjoyed' that he was unwilling to sell.

Meantime, thus driven back upon himself, he gave his idle hours to building an even grander mansion in which we can wander to-day and see a richer collection of portraits than that which made Clarendon House the envy of all contemporaries.

The History of the Rebellion, as mere writing, leaves much to be desired. It is not readable. The course of the story is clogged with ill-digested material, letters, petitions, despatches, statutes. Toward the end these diminish in number and the action becomes more closely knit and vigorous. There are in the later volumes many bits of swift and vivid narrative, notably the admirable account of Charles the Second's escape after the battle of Worcester. Still, to make any continuous and steady progress in the book requires a reader of patience and perseverance. Even in the great battle-pieces the historian is by no means at his best. They are confused, slow, lacking intense and salient situations. Now and then a gorgeous high light strikes a fair head or a glittering cuirass, but the general course of things is lost in smoke.

A NATURALIST OF SOULS

For Clarendon has not only the Elizabethan
cumbrousness in the conduct of his story, he has
the Elizabethan inarticulateness. He may have
known Dryden, if he condescended to look down so
far. He knew nothing of that inimitable march of
common prose which Dryden learned from French
clarity and native wit. Clarendon has often Milton's
grandeur. He also has too often Milton's heaviness
and a trailing incoherence outdoing Milton's. He
himself accuses Selden of 'a little undervaluing the
beauty of style and too much propensity to the
language of antiquity.' But to eyes of the twentieth
century his own writing seems liable to the same
accusation. He has sentences of a singular, haunting gravity and beauty: 'He had no ambition of title
or office or preferment, but only to be kindly looked
upon and kindly spoken to and quietly to enjoy his
own fortune.' He has many others which an American school-boy would be ashamed of, like this wandering concatenation of relatives: 'The Prince left
a strong garrison there that brought almost all that
whole country into contribution, which was a great
enlargement to the King's quarters, which now,
without interruption, extended from Oxford to
Worcester, which important city, with the other
of Hereford and those counties, had before been

quitted by the rebels.' It may be said that such faults should be overlooked in a great writer, but it is precisely because of them that the modern general reader shuns Clarendon and knows nothing of him.

In his political and philosophical view of human affairs at large Clarendon is distinctly a moderate, even a liberal. He prefers the old constitution and traditions of England. He has no love for the extreme vagaries of Puritans in religion or for republicans in matters of state. Yet no one appreciates more clearly than he the errors and excesses of Stuart absolutism, even before the Restoration: 'I pray God the almighty justice be not angry with and weary of the government of kings and princes, for it is a strange declension monarchical government is fallen to, in the opinion of the common people within these later years.'

It is not, however, with Clarendon's attitude toward life in general that we are here concerned, but with his portrayal of men and women, of the human heart. Though we employ to some extent the phraseology of painting, it is essential to realize the difference between the two methods of representation which Lessing long ago discussed so fruitfully. Lines and colors give us at once the individual face. This words can never do. You may analyze features, you may dissect expressions, you may pile detail upon detail. But the more you elaborate, the further you get from unity of effect. The more you charge memory with particular outlines, the less you succeed in producing a complete, definite, permanent image. 'The description of a face is a needless thing, as it never conveys a true idea,' says Lady Mary Montagu, curtly, but in the main justly. No. The art of the word painter is suggestion. Take, in a little different field, the line of Keats,

'Fast-fading violets covered up in leaves.'

The landscape artist can render the violets peeping from their leafy covert with infinite delicacy and grace. What he can never render, except as he finds a willing spirit to interpret, is the poet's comment, the world of reflection and emotion contained in the epithet, 'fast-fading.' So with the portrayal of men. The cunning artist who has only words at his disposal will not delay long in trying to convey exactness and completeness of lineament. He will strike out some quick touch of feeling, some hint of passion, some profound association of thought, or achievement, or desire. This will not always be confined to the spiritual world. It may be intensely physical. But the effect will be an effect of suggestion, not of reproduction. That is the essential point. Thus Shakespeare gives Cassius 'a lean and hungry look,' and Milton's Satan appears not 'less than archangel ruined and the excess of glory obscured.' Thus Tacitus depicts Otho 'stretching out kind hands, flattering the mob, flinging kisses, doing all things like a slave that he might rule all things.' Thus Saint-Simon strikes off one of his minor figures, tumbling body and soul together in passionate hurly-burly: 'She was starched, made up, always embarrassed, a wit scarce natural, an affected devotion, full of outwardness and odd fashions; in two words, nothing amiable, nothing sociable, nothing natural; tall, straight, an air which wished to impose, yet to be gentle; austere and distinctly verging on the bitter-sweet. No one could get on with her, and she could get on with nothing and nobody. She was charmed to have done with it all and go, and no one had the slightest desire to detain her.' Whoever reads Clarendon faithfully will see that in this art of suggestion, of stimulating the imagination, he is one of the richest, the mightiest, the most fruitful of all the great masters of words.

The chief danger which besets the painter of soul

is rhetoric. Words are his instruments. He must keep them bright and polished, must get from them all their resources of music and power, study them, profit by them always with fertile variety and endless inspiration. But they must be his servants, not his masters. He must make all this use of them by instinct, as it were; for his eyes, his thoughts, his whole heart, must be always on his subject. He must be penetrated by it, wrapt in it; it must speak right through him and dominate all his powers of expression in instinctive service. The instant we feel that he is thinking more of his effects than of his characters, that tricks of speech are more to him than secrets of soul, that instant we lose our confidence. He may amuse, he will rarely inspire.

Of course every writer has his rhetorical moments. There are turns in Tacitus, turns in Saint-Simon, that one could wish away. When Clarendon says of the Earl of Arundel that 'he resorted sometimes to the court because there only was a greater man than himself, and went thither the seldomer because there was a greater man than himself,' we feel that he is even more anxious to show Clarendon's cleverness than Arundel's vanity. But in the really great soul-painters these slips are rare, because their passion for human truth engrosses them beyond anything else. In lesser men the passion for human truth is a less serious matter. Macaulay's 'History of England' is as rapid, as brilliant, as absorbing as a well-constructed drama. If only one could rid one's self of the impression that one is watching a clever variety actor doing tricks!

What interests Clarendon is not tricks, but men. To be sure, with him as with Saint-Simon the gift lies quite as much in imaginative portrayal as in moral insight. It is the new word, the old words used new ways, the significant touch, the illuminating flash. But the difference from Macaulay is simply that the other two think of the subject first, of the word only second, if at all.

Nor do I wish to imply that Clarendon's insight is less than his imagination. He could not have painted if he had not seen. The fine secrets, the deeper places of the human heart, are open to him. Gardiner refers to 'his usual habit of blundering,' and altogether treats him with a good deal of contempt as a rather pompous, rather conventional, rather timid, and eminently legal sort of personage. Warburton, Clarendon's earliest commentator, speaks differently: 'In the knowledge of human nature (the noblest qualification of the historian) this great author excels all the Greek and Latin historians put together.' This is strong language, but the 'History' and 'Life' go far to justify it. Personally Clarendon had his foibles (Saint-Simon even more so), but I think most of us had rather blunder immortally with him than be mortally accurate and commonplace with the industrious Gardiner.

Although Clarendon does his work always with conscientious earnestness, this does not mean that he puts no humor into it. Like Saint-Simon, he saw the oddities, the farcical contrasts between human infirmity and human greatness. Like Saint-Simon, he expressed them with an intense, incisive vigor which makes us sigh even as we smile, or, if you prefer, the other way about. Sometimes, indeed, his humor, like Pepys's, is unintentional, as when he speaks of 'Colonel d'Ews, a young man of notable courage and vivacity, who had his leg shot off by a cannon bullet, of which he speedily and very cheerfully died.' More often he smiles himself and lets the reader see that he does, though briefly and with compressed lip, as befits a chancellor and one weighted with the charge of state affairs —

'Silent smiles, the gravity of mirth,'

as a poet of that day calls them. Now it is a dry comment on some solemn scene, like that on Blake's funeral, recalling Voltaire's remark that Admiral Byng was shot *pour encourager les autres:* 'He wanted no pomp of funeral when he was dead, Cromwell causing him to be brought up by land to London in all the state that could be; and, according to the method of that time, to encourage his officers to be killed, that they might be pompously buried, he was, with all the solemnity possible, and at the charge of the public, interred in Harry the Seventh's chapel, among the monuments of the kings.' Now it is a witty, if cynical, epigram, dissecting the heart or brain of some great personage, as of the Earl of Arundel: 'He did not love the Scots; he did not love the Puritans, which good qualities were allayed by another negative; he did love nobody else.'

In accordance with what I have said above as to the limits of word portraiture, Clarendon is cautious in his attempt to depict physical characteristics. He is much more conservative here than Saint-Simon, who has cruel words for immortalizing ugliness, as in his sketch of Mézières: 'Humped both before and behind, his head in his chest far down below his shoulders, hurting you to watch him breathe; mere bones, moreover, and a yellow face that looked like a frog's.' Clarendon has nothing of this kind. Yet he has a rough vigor of his own in dealing with the earthly frame of even royal personages. Of James the First's death he says: He 'fell into a quartan ague, which meeting many humors in a fat, unwieldy body of fifty-four years, in four or five fits carried him out of the world.' When soul is to be read by body, he has subtle observations often, as in the case of Sir Henry Vane: 'He had an unusual aspect, which, though it might naturally proceed from both father and mother, neither of which were beautiful persons, yet made men think there was somewhat in him of extraordinary; and his whole life made good that imagination.' And equally so when soul is not to be read by body, but masks foul evil under bodily simplicity: 'He (Goring) could help himself with all the insinuations of doubt, or fear, or shame, or simplicity in his face that might gain belief to a greater degree than I ever saw any man; and could seem the most confounded when he was best prepared, and the most out of countenance when he was best resolved, and to want words and the habit of speaking when they flowed from no man with greater power.' Few writers have ever painted more vividly the mighty influence of the soul over the body. Thus Falkland, after the peace between King and Commons was at last broken, 'grew into a perfect habit of uncheerfulness; and he who had been so exactly unreserved and affable to all men that his face and countenance was always present, and vacant to his company, and held any cloudiness and less pleasantness of the visage a kind of rudeness and incivility, became on a sudden less communicable and thence very sad, pale, and exceedingly affected with the spleen.'

If we wish to compare two great English word-painters in this matter of physical description, we can take Clarendon and Burnet on Lauderdale. Clarendon, like Rembrandt, prefers suggestion, atmosphere, touches the gross, material singularity with vigor, but with speed. 'The fatness of his tongue that ever filled his mouth.' Burnet, with the flat, brusque energy of Hals, dwells on ugly detail till it takes almost the proportion of monstrosity: 'He made a very ill appearance; he was very big; his hair red, hanging oddly about him; his tongue was too big for his mouth, which made him bedew all he talked to.'

It is by these brief touches, in both the physical and moral world, that a great artist gets often his most lasting effects, impressions that fix themselves upon the memory and recur immortally, not only in association with that special character, but with others whom they fit and illuminate. Here no one has ever equalled Tacitus, whether in the familiar bits, 'he would have been thought of all men the most worthy to reign if he had never reigned'; or in those less known: 'He could squander, but he could not give'; 'he gave, but sparingly, and not as one about to die.'

Amplitude, not brevity, is Clarendon's distinguishing characteristic. Yet when he chooses, he can fling one sentence at a man that will stick to him forever. 'Wilmot was of a haughty and ambitious nature, of a pleasant wit, and an ill understanding, as never considering above one thing at once; but he considered that one thing so impatiently that he did not admit anything else to be worth consideration.' Cowley 'had an extraordinary kindness for Mr. Hyde (Clarendon himself) till he found he betook himself to business which he believed ought never to be preferred before his company.' Selden 'would have hindered them (the Parliament), if he could, with his own safety, to which he was always enough indulgent.' Saint Albans 'had that kindness for himself that he thought everybody did believe him.'

The historian is more at ease, however, when he takes a little wider sweep. To enumerate, or even to suggest, the elaborate, splendid portraits which fill page after page of both the 'Life' and the 'History' would be altogether impossible. Will not some one some day pay Clarendon the deserved honor of isolating these from the clogging context, as has been done most successfully in the very similar case of Saint-Simon?

I will at least quote a single specimen, not perhaps one of the most alluring, but finely representative, the full-length of Cottington taken after his death: 'He was a very wise man, by the great and long experience he had in business of all kinds; and by his natural temper, which was not liable to any transport of anger or any other passion, but could bear contradiction and even reproach without being moved or put out of his way, for he was very steady in pursuing what he proposed to himself, and had a courage not to be frighted or amazed with any opposition. . . . He lived very nobly, well served, and attended in his house, had a better stable of horses, better provision for sports (especially of hawks, in which he took great delight), than most of his quality, and lived always with great splendor; for though he loved money very well, and did not warily enough consider the circumstances of getting it, he spent it well all ways but in giving, which he did not affect. He was of an excellent humor, and very easy to live with; and under a grave countenance, covered the most of mirth, and caused more than any man of the most pleasant disposition. He never used anybody ill, but used many very well for whom he had no regard: his greatest fault was that he could dissemble and make men believe that he loved them very well, when he cared not for them. He had not very tender affections, nor bowels apt to yearn at all objects which deserved compassion: he was heartily weary of the world, and no man was more willing to die, which is an argument that he had peace of conscience. He left behind him a greater esteem of his parts, than love to his person.'

If it be inferred from this and some of my other quotations that Clarendon painted common or unlovely natures best, it may be answered that he lived amid the shock of fierce ambitions and cruel selfishnesses, and for contrast the reader may turn to the much longer and exquisite study of Falkland and to some others in the beginning of the Life.

It will be asked, how far was the painter influenced by his own prejudices in painting both dark and bright? Every man is influenced by them; but he, I think, not much further than most of us would be in writing of our own contemporaries. Human character is an unstable thing, an ample, shifting thing, altering with every angle of vision, like a far mountain or a summer cloud. Therefore no study of it is final. Only, that made by a man of genius is rich in suggestion and permanent in beauty. When Clarendon analyzes Hampden and Cromwell, we know that we must allow something for cropped crown and steeple-hat. When he says of the Earls of Pembroke and Salisbury that 'they had rather the King and his posterity should be destroyed than that Wilton should be taken from the one of them or Hatfield from the other; the preservation of both which from any danger they both believed to be the highest point of prudence and politic circumspection,' we have to remember that these were Parliamentary commissioners. Likewise the praise of Laud, aptly mingled with shrewd blame, is such as befits the august head of the Episcopal Church. And in the summing-up of the whole matter of Charles I we admire the historian's ingenuity rather more than his judgment: 'If he were not the best King, if he were without some parts and qualities which have made some kings great and happy, no other prince was ever unhappy who was possessed of half his virtues and endowments and so much without any kind of vice.'

What I miss most in Clarendon, considering the extent of his portraiture, is any elaborate study of women. Did he respect them too much, or fear them too much, or despise them too much? Of his own first wife, who died young, he says: 'He bore her loss with so great passion and confusion of spirit that it shook all the frame of his resolution.' Doubtless out of compliment to her memory, he soon married a second 'with whom he lived very comfortably in the most uncomfortable times and very joyfully in those times when matter of joy was administered.' Perhaps he thought the privacy of the sex should be considered, even in an age when they did not much consider it themselves.

He certainly did not approve of feminine interference in politics. 'There being at that time,' he says of the early, better days, 'no ladies who had disposed themselves to intermeddle in business'; and, later, of the difficulty of managing the court at Oxford, 'the town being full of lords and many persons of the best quality, with very many ladies, who were not easily pleased and kept others from being so.' His most bitter opponent under his first master was the Queen, and under his second the royal mistress. Yet of neither has he left any such finished picture as of his male friends and enemies.

How different is this from the way of Tacitus, who touches so many women, briefly, as in everything, but masterfully, like the wife of Vitellius, *ultra feminam ferox*. How different especially from Saint-Simon, whose pages swarm with women, delightful or hideous — the Duchesse de Bourgogne, the Duchesse du Maine, the Princesse des Ursins, a hundred others, and, above all, Madame de Maintenon, whom he detested as Clarendon did Lady Castlemaine, but did not therefore refrain from painting in every light and in every shadow. Madame de Maintenon, 'whose passion it was to know everything, to meddle in everything, to govern everything.' Madame de Maintenon, 'who for kinship's sake loved those who had repented much better than those who had nothing of which to repent.'

Surely Clarendon's opportunities for studying women were no less than Saint-Simon's. He saw two queens daily, and their ladies, high and low. Doubtless he understood them, or thought he did. But he makes little attempt to have us understand them. Only rarely does he throw off a careless sug-

gestion of some minor figure. There is Mademoi-
selle de Longueville, who 'was looked upon as one
of the greatest and richest marriages in France in
respect of her fortune; in respect of her person not
at all attractive, being a lady of a very low stature,
and that stature no degree straight.' There is Lady
Monk, 'a woman of the lowest extraction, least wit,
and less beauty, who, taking no care for any other
part of herself, had deposited her soul with some
Presbyterian ministers, who disposed her to that interest.' There is the wife of Prince Rupert, who,
'from the time she had the first intimation that the
King had designed her husband for the command of
the fleet, was all storm and fury; and according to
the modesty of her nature poured out a thousand
full-mouthed curses against all who had contributed
to that counsel, . . . but the company she kept and
the conversation she was accustomed to could not
propagate the reproaches far; and the poor General
felt them most, who knew the Chancellor to be his
very faithful and firm friend, and that he would not
be less so because his wife was no wiser than she was
born to be.'

Also, as compared with Saint-Simon, it seems to
me that Clarendon is less successful in depicting
groups of figures — that is, great historical scenes

and critical situations. He has, indeed, some that are very striking; the death of Buckingham, the arrest of Charles I, the humiliation of the Second Buckingham, the death of Falkland. But he sometimes fails when we expect him at his best. For instance, the trial of Charles is passed over very lightly. And he has nowhere anything that approaches the great scenes of Saint-Simon, such as the feeding of the carp or the deaths of Monseigneur and the Duc de Bourgogne.

I end by asking myself what was Clarendon's motive in his immense undertaking. 'If,' he says in one passage, 'the celebrating the memory of eminent and extraordinary persons and transmitting their great virtues to posterity be one of the principal ends and duties of history. . . .' No doubt he thought it was so, and labored valiantly for that object. But a great painter likes to immortalize himself as well as others, takes legitimate delight in the skillful touches of his art. Clarendon must have found in his own and others' word-painting the keen pleasure which Saint-Simon displayed so naïvely on hearing of a clever saying of Louis XIV's: 'When Maréchal told me this, I was overcome with astonishment at so fine a stroke of the brush.'

Also Clarendon must have had the passion for studying mankind, though he is conservative, as always, in the expression of it: 'I was at that time no stranger to the persons of most that governed and a diligent observer of their carriage.' This is sober compared even to the frankness of Pepys: 'And I, as I am in all things curious,' let alone the inquisitive fury of Saint-Simon: 'This fact is not important, but it is amusing. It is especially significant with a prince as serious and as imposing as Louis XIV; and all these little court anecdotes are well worth while.' 'I skimmed off a few of these details on the spot.' 'For me, I glutted myself with the spectacle.' Yet Clarendon unquestionably derived immense pleasure from his rich opportunities for reading 'bare soul.'

And with all his experience of what was dark and evil, I do not think his observation was unkindly. He could be cruel with the cruel and cynical with the cynical, but he retained more of human tenderness than Saint-Simon; more, much more than that other masterly English painter, John, Lord Hervey.

Clarendon had, indeed, honestly tried to do his best for his country. He had been deceived, betrayed, mocked, slandered, ruined, exiled. What wonder that he summed up his knowledge of the world with a little bitterness. 'He had originally in his nature so great a tenderness and love towards all mankind that he . . . did really believe all men were such as they appeared to be. . . . These unavoidable reflections first made him discern how weak and foolish all his imaginations had been and how blind a surveyor he had been of the inclinations and affections of the heart of man (and of) this world, where whatsoever is good and desirable suddenly perisheth and nothing is lasting but the folly and wickedness of the inhabitants thereof.'

It was on a dark day in a sad, strange land that he wrote that. Nevertheless, his great books show everywhere the desire for what is noble and of good report; nay, more, the real, lasting love of his fellow men, not only as they might be, but as they actually are, which remains, I think, the firmest secret of human felicity.

1911

X
A GENTLEMAN OF ATHENS

X

A GENTLEMAN OF ATHENS

XENOPHON was born in Athens and grew up there; but at the close of the fifth century Athenian glory had gone by, and when about thirty, he left his native city, not to return, at any rate for many years.

After his departure, he led at first a brilliantly active life, strenuous almost beyond modern possibility, seeing strange people and doing strange things. Then he settled down on a country estate, of his own, where, in the pleasant words of his ancient biographer, 'he passed his time hunting, entertaining his friends, and writing history.' I do not know how he could have passed it more agreeably. He himself says of the farmer's life that a man who is free to choose cannot pick out any other so delightful.

Being a Greek, and therefore an instinctive artist, he could both do things and describe them. 'He was called the Attic Muse for his sweetness of speech,' says the same biographer, most sweetly. He is a little garrulous, a little prolix, has not the

259

concentrated energy of Thucydides. But for narrating great matters in a flowing, candid fashion, not many have surpassed him. Grace and purity of outline are surely among preëminent Attic qualities. They are Xenophon's. His simplicity has not Voltaire's incisive point. It has the unfailing charm of natural ease which belongs to George Sand and Renan.

The horrors of the Athenian plague or the slow agony of that Sicilian downfall, as rendered by Thucydides, would have been entirely beyond the pitch of Xenophon as a writer. But he has most spirited battle-pieces in both 'Cyropædia' and 'Hellenica.' The hunting scene, in the essay on that subject, moves with a vim and gusto that Trollope cannot surpass, and this is to praise highly. In a very different vein, what could be more winning, more nobly winning, than the love story of Abradatas and Panthea in the 'Cyropædia'? Panthea, separated from her husband, resists the ardent suit of Araspes, is reunited to her husband with ecstacy, and when he is slain in battle, kills herself upon his grave. On the other hand, passages of heroic feeling between man and man are frequent, as the fine exchange of honorable enmity and friendship between Agesilaus and Pharnabazus in the

'Hellenica.' And Xenophon occasionally reports, or invents, a saying as memorable as those of Plutarch. 'The pilot of Callicratidas observed to him that it might be well to sail away; for the Athenians had a good many more ships than he had. But Callicratidas answered that Sparta would be none the worse off, if he died, but to flee was a shameful thing.'

Personally Xenophon was a man of good-humored equipoise and of a wide joy in the surface of life. He had not the passionate curiosity of Herodotus; but he noted with interest and accuracy the manners and habits of the people he met, not only Persians and Carduchians, but the daily people about him, Greek men and women, high and low, lovers and haters. When he finally settled down in the country, he studied country things lovingly, farm ways and farm management, dogs and horses and the creatures that his dogs and horses helped him hunt. His discussion of the horse is as minute as an auctioneer's or Shakespeare's in 'Venus and Adonis,' but it is far from being dull. On the contrary, it shows a keen sympathy with horses and riders both. Let mane and tail grow, he says. The tail is useful to keep off flies, and the mane is handy to hold on to. And again:

'In mounting, raise the body with the left hand. Then, stretching out the right, swing yourself up, keeping the leg bent under (to avoid an awkward appearance from the rear). Do not rest the knee on the horse's back, but fling the thigh clear over against the other side.'

In more serious and deeper matters of the soul also, Xenophon was an observer, though perhaps not a very profound one. I do not know that any classical writer has left a more charming picture of the Greek wife than he draws in his essay on household economy. It is as full of shrewd turns as of reverence and tenderness. Thus, for shrewdness: 'Since it is the woman's province to save things already got, the deity, knowing that to thrift a little fear is no bad helper, made the woman by nature more timid than the man.' And for reverence, a husband thus addresses his wife: 'But the sweetest thing of all is that if you show yourself finer natured than I and lead me to be your servant, you need never fear that the passage of time will make you neglected, but you may be sure that as you grow more and more the companion of me and of your children and the guardian of your home, the more you will be honored in it.' Which suggests Cowper's verses:

A GENTLEMAN OF ATHENS

'For still to love, though pressed with ill,
In wintry age to feel no chill,
With me is to be lovely still,
    My Mary.'

It is, however, the ideal wife who is here dealt
with; and from this fact as well as from the re-
mainder of the essay, it is easy to surmise the weakness of Xenophon's observation. He was essentially
an idealist and saw things as he wished to see them.
When he depicts a historical figure like Agesilaus,
he evidently draws him as he ought to have been
rather than as he was. The characters of the generals in the 'Anabasis' are, indeed, cut with firm
sharpness of outline; but Xenophon had rubbed
against them too closely to make it possible for him
to overlook the facts. As soon as he can allow himself a little perspective, he poses, arranges, trans-
figures, to get his effect.

For he was a born moralist, in fact a preacher,
in fact, to use a lamentable word for an estima-
ble thing, an educator, by instinct and training.
Socrates got hold of him young; and just because
he had less than Socrates of pure spiritual curiosity,
he had more of the mania of making the world over
according to his theories. Whether he was really
practical in common matters I do not know, though

the 'Anabasis' would lead one to suspect it. When he settled down on the farm, could he mend a hinge and plane a door for Mrs. Xenophon, or patch up the little Xenophons' broken toys and set them working again? Or did he leave these things to the slaves and himself live in a world of practical dreams, telling long stories of Socrates's wisdom, boring the aforesaid lady and causing the little Xenophons to wink at one another decorously? Certain it is, at any rate, that he had a strong inclination towards pointing out how life should be conducted. He was modest about it, simple about it, but very much in earnest.

Thus, the 'Memorabilia' is less a biography of Socrates than a manual of conduct, a very persuasive, winning manual, because the writer is not austere, severe, but full of gentleness and human kindness. Indeed, this gentleness in Xenophon is most noticeable and attractive, especially as he was so much a man of action, fire, and movement.

As an educator, he was the first to write a Rollo book, be it to his credit or not. His Rollo was called Cyrus and was king of Persia, but he had the ideal characteristics of his inimitable New England successor. He did all those things he ought to have done, left undone all those things he ought not to have done, had abounding health in him as the reward of virtue, and was always imperturbably ready with the aptest of platitudes. At home he was accustomed to a rather Spartan diet. When he visited his grandfather, the old gentleman was naturally anxious to make things pleasant and provided the table with goodies to an unlimited extent. All he got in return was: 'Grandpa, what a bother your meals must be, if you have to reach for all these dishes and taste so many kinds of drinks.' 'What!' says grandpa. 'Don't you find this much better than your food at home?' 'Oh, no,' says Rollo. 'The road to repletion is much simpler and easier with us than with you. Bread and meat take us right where we wish to go; but you are going to the same place, and yet you travel a long way about before you get there.' Imagine a royal grandfather more exquisitely crushed.

And what interests us, so-called Christians, coming two thousand years after, is not so much how successfully he preaches, as the fact that he does preach. Viewed as history or biography, the 'Cyropædia' is absurd. No king, no man, was ever so inimitably perfect as its hero. But that a Greek, four centuries before Christ, should conceive so noble and Christian an ideal of patience, of sympathy, of generosity, of self-control and self-sacrifice, is much more worthy of attention than the facts about the real Cyrus would have been.

Furthermore, two things save the 'Cyropædia' from being a mere Sunday-School book. First, its grace. It is written with the ease and the perfection of Fénelon. We may have to look elsewhere for Greek grandeur. But Greek naïveté and Greek charm have few better examples.

And then, though Xenophon was too earnest and too shallow to be an Aristophanes, he had his own sense of fun and mingles pleasantry with grace in a fashion, for a preacher, very surprising and comforting. His best production in this kind is the little dialogue called the 'Symposium,' certainly less lofty and less airy than Plato's, but full of gayety, swift mirth, and witty retort, with sound wisdom behind it. In the 'Cyropædia' also, there is plenty of laughter, or broad smiles; and if you assert that this is utterly incompatible with Rollo, I shall not deny it. But Rollo is there just the same. Indeed, if we may compare very ancient things with very modern, the atmosphere of human kindness (*bonté*, as the French express it, untranslatably) drenched with sunshine, which pervades the whole book, recalls, at a considerable distance, the

266

'Abbé Constantin' of Halévy. It is impossible to revive in translation such long dead merriment, but I may at least refer to one or two instances. Gobryas offers riches and his charming daughter to Cyrus, if Cyrus will aid him to obtain vengeance. Cyrus, in declining the reward, jestingly expresses thanks for an opportunity, such as falls to few men, of showing that his virtue is of a kind that can withstand temptation. Again, a devoted but grumbling follower complains that another is more favored than he. 'Because,' says Cyrus, 'he not only does what I bid him, but does it with delight and takes more pleasure in my good fortune than in his own.' 'Ah,' says the grumbler, 'I will do as he does. But how shall I show my pleasure, by laughing, by clapping my hands?' 'You might dance the war-dance,' suggests a sympathetic bystander. And they all fall a-laughing together. Xenophon's own pleasant comment on Persian degeneration is also worth remembrance. In old times, he says, they boasted that they ate only one meal a day. So they do now — but it lasts from sunrise to sunset.

As Xenophon had definite ideas about ethics in general, so he had his political opinions, which are characteristically interesting. He was born and bred under the democracy of Athens, and, perhaps for that reason, did not think very highly of it; as many Americans to-day, living so near to our cumbrous governmental machinery that they hear all its creaks and gasps and groans, look fondly at the paternal systems of Europe, which seem to work with grand perfection — at a distance. Xenophon wrote a little essay on the constitution of Sparta, in which he gives it distinctly the advantage as compared with that of Athens. And elsewhere in his works he expresses the same opinion, speaking of the Spartan oligarchy as 'the best of all government.' Nay, his love of order, of discipline, of authority, led him to admire even the absolutism of Persia, viewed under an ideal light, as he viewed everything. Indeed, it is most curious to see how, Greek as he was, manly, simple, and straightforward as he was, he yet felt the charm of Persian pomp, parade, and show. In the 'Cyropædia' he dwells lovingly on the elaborate details of his hero's triumphal progress, the marchings, and the banners, and the bendings, and the salutations, things one would think most repugnant to a son of free Athens. But it seems to be in much the same spirit as that in which a child piles up wonders in a fairy story.

A GENTLEMAN OF ATHENS

There is one most striking passage in the essay on the government of the Athenians — probably not Xenophon's but close enough to his opinions — in which the writer lets loose all his wrath against the abuses of democracy. It is the language of a man utterly wearied out with the blatancy of politicians and the cunning rhetoric of demagogues who play upon the passions of the mob for their own purposes, and the conclusion is that government should be given not to the rabble, but to the good, the honest, and the trustworthy.

Strange, is it not? that the writer's doctrinaire idealism prevents him from seeing the truth which stares forth from even this distorted statement and which makes some of us still ready to live and die with democracy, for all its faults. Who are the good, who are the honest, who are the trustworthy? Those whom you, or I, or Xenophon pick out? A class, that is. And every class, however honest, will legislate for itself first, precisely as this writer says, for the rabble — and may not you, or I, or Xenophon, be the rabble? — only afterwards. Here is the best of all defenses — from the mouth of an adversary — of that clumsy, blundering monster of democracy which must save the world, if the world is ever to be saved.

A NATURALIST OF SOULS

With speculative philosophy Xenophon concerns himself much less than with politics. He consorted with metaphysicians, but I fancy he had not much taste for them, nor they for him. Indeed, it is easy to imagine Plato's grave irony and Aristophanes's open ridicule in regard to this honest, earnest, but somewhat conventional gentleman who sedulously frequented wisdom without an entire comprehension of her subtlest mysteries. Yet it is a great gain that the Socrates of Plato's fine-spun syllogizing should be also reflected for us in Xenophon's homely record which always keeps an eye to the practical and the dusty things of every day. A Boswell, you urge, and with some justice. But a minutely observing Boswell has his usefulness, and perhaps sticks closer to the actual life of portraiture than more original genius.

How attractive, how simple, how really gospel-like is the old biographer's account of the disciple's becoming acquainted with his master: 'They say that Socrates first met him in a narrow place, and thrusting his staff before him, hindered him from going on. And Socrates asked him where things needful were to be bought. And he answered and told him. And again he asked him where good men were to be found. And he could not tell. Then

Socrates said unto him, "Follow me and learn."
And after that he became a disciple of Socrates.'

Something also is there of gospel sternness, of
gospel aptness, and of gospel grace in the various
logia which Xenophon records with the naïve simplicity of Mark or Matthew: 'Some one complained
that the drinking water was very warm. And he
answered him, "When thou wishest to bathe, it
will be as thou wishest it." ' 'A man chastised his
servant very harshly. And Socrates said unto him:
"Why art thou angry with thy servant?" And the
man answered, "Because, although a huge feeder,
he is slothful, and although most greedy for money,
he will not work." And Socrates said, "Hast thou
considered which is the more deserving of stripes,
thou or he?"'

And if Xenophon was no great theologian, he
was surely one of the most sweetly, most whole-
somely religious natures that ever lived. Matthew
Arnold, with exquisite justice, called Spenser the
ideal Puritan. Xenophon, I think, might be called
the ideal Puritan also. No treader of Plymouth
Rock saw God's finger more present in his everyday
affairs than did this Greek of two thousand years
ago, or strove more highly and more holily to mould
everyday affairs in accordance with what he be-

lieved to be the divine will. Only for Xenophon, the Greek, who lived always in sunshine, the divine will could not mean things harsh, things bitter, things austere, but was infinitely compatible with love, with laughter, and with joy. 'For whatsoever things are done with the aid of God, such things must surely be prosperous and fortunate.'

It is true that Xenophon's constant recurrence to the divine, his oracles, his auguries, his sacrifices, seem to us now superstitious, not to say laughable. Something doubtless we have gained here, something also we have lost. Any one who surveys 'great, avaricious, sensual, pleasure-loving America' in the light of past ages and vanished beliefs, will, I think, be struck most of all with the absence of God — I mean, of just that vital sense of the divine activity and omnipresence which in Xenophon is so significant. We have relegated God to the cold shadow of our rarely visited churches; and even there, between the encroachments of apologetic theology and the chatter of social service, He finds a scant abiding place. Xenophon's religion is alive and warm at least, even if it is fit only for childish minds.

And observe that his superstition, if primitive, is neither cowering nor unmanly. He consults the gods about all action because he believes that the gods made man and are ready to bestow their wisdom upon him, if he invokes them rightly. But he believes also, with all his heart, that the Sabbath was made for man, not man for the Sabbath. His devotion is practical, sane, healthy, and looks to a useful life in this world as well as to a seemly reverence for the other. I like especially his shrewd conduct upon setting out with the expedition of Cyrus. Socrates advised him to consult the oracle as to whether he should go or not. Xenophon immediately consulted the oracle — but as to how he should go most successfully, taking the main question for granted. And Socrates reproved him; but I imagine Socrates was inwardly amused and gratified.

Lest it should be inferred from this that Xenophon's religion had anything insincere about it, let me quote a passage from the 'Cyropædia' as impressive in its sincerity as it is grand in its spiritual purport. Cyrus enjoins upon his successors his commands for their future guidance: 'If, therefore, it is as I conceive and the soul leaves the body behind it, then, out of love for my soul, do those things which I bid you. But if it is not so, and if the soul remains in the body and dies when the body dies, yet out of love for the gods who live forever, and behold all things, and have power over all things, who sustain this universal order unvexed, unwearied, unerring, unutterable in grandeur and in majesty — out of love for these, let not your action nor your thought be ever unworthy or profane.'

So far it has been interesting to see this sweet and noble nature in study and reflection; but to see it in deeds is more interesting still. For the man was born for deeds and felt himself to be so. With the frankness characteristic of a Greek, and especially of him, he confesses his desire for distinction and glory. 'Praise is the sweetest of all sounds,' Pliny quotes from him; but the turn of this is more like Pliny than Xenophon, whose language elsewhere is at once more dignified and more passionate: 'There are souls which long for glory as others do for food and drink.'

And so, in his ripest manhood, he went with his friend Proxenus to join the army with which the younger Cyrus was preparing to wrest the Persian throne from his brother Artaxerxes. Ten thousand Greeks there were, sound in muscle, stubborn in courage, full, like Xenophon, of Greek ardor, Greek laughter, and Greek curiosity. A handful of their forefathers had crushed the hordes of Darius and Xerxes, when they came swarming over sea. Why should not the no less valiant sons return the visit?

They did, not at first aspiring to overthrow an empire, but merely hired, as they thought, for some minor plundering expedition, which would fill their stomachs and their pockets and their no less greedy eyes, and give something to talk about by winter firesides in pleasant Greece.

Then Cyrus lured them on, with pay and promise and persuasion, till suddenly they found themselves confronted by Artaxerxes and the whole Persian army, far outnumbering, not only the petty band of Greeks, but all the followers of Cyrus together. And the Greeks remembered Marathon and charged gayly and found it as easy in Asia as it was in Europe. Down went the stately horsemen before them, and the motley footmen of all nations; and the dreaded scythe-chariots swept through opened ranks, causing more laughter than injury. But though they conquered, Cyrus was killed; and there they were, left alone, only ten thousand, in a strange land, among millions of enemies. It was enough to break the light-heartedness of even Greeks.

It did not break theirs. The leaders took counsel together, kept their ranks in order and sharp watch, played a shrewd game of diplomacy with the treacherous barbarians, and made it seem almost as if a little knot of unsupported invaders might dictate terms to the whole Persian empire. Then they went astray, trusted where there was nothing to trust, were betrayed, captured — and vanished. One night the ten thousand found themselves, by the loss of all their higher officers, transformed from an army into a mob of waifs and strays.

And here was the chance of Xenophon. He was no general, no officer, only a friend of Proxenus who had vanished with the rest. But he valued his life as much as any general. In Athens, whose free speech he detested, he had learned to use his tongue, to tell men what they ought to do and how to do it. A leader, they must have leaders. He was not asking the position. Let some one else lead, and he would follow. But leaders they must have, and then all would be well.

So they chose leaders, Cheirisophus and others besides Xenophon, but Xenophon was the soul of it; and out of the center of Persia, over wide rivers and high mountains, through barren deserts and snowdrifts, through enemies who fought them with everything, from fair speeches to stones, they made their way back to a Greek-speaking country, not indeed ten thousand, but so many as to make us wonder at what Greek training and Greek courage and Greek endurance must have been.

But we are interested in Xenophon, not in ten thousand Greeks, in the wonderful narrative of all his adventures and experiences, and in what it reveals to us of the man himself. Of course, we must remember that we have only his own story. If Cheirisophus had kept a journal, things might have appeared otherwise. But the most winning thing in Xenophon's book is his entire modesty. He keeps himself out of sight, or if by chance he takes part in some great action, it is narrated dispassionately, remotely, as if the hero were some one else. There is not one of the many personal memoirs of our own Civil War that gives a more attractive impression of its author than the relation of Xenophon; and some of them show a self-seeking and self-justification from which he is entirely free. Yet all the more for this self-effacement do his high qualities stand out on every page.

To begin with, he was brave, not uselessly, but splendidly brave. If a forlorn hope was to be headed or an example to be set, Xenophon was there. And his energy was equal to his bravery. In that march one misfortune seemed to hurry on

the track of another. Now provisions failed, now
the light-armed enemy kept out of reach but near
enough to injure, now a pass was closed in front,
or an unfordable river suddenly crossed the path.
But Xenophon had always some device ready, or
found some other man that had, or filled the whole
army with cheerfulness, till fortune — God, he
would have said — supplied the need or smoothed
the difficulty.

It is interesting to follow his relations with other
commanders, notably with Cheirisophus. The
latter was a Lacedemonian and his kind were no
more liked in Greece than Prussians in Germany.
They were an immense reliance in trouble, but
they were harsh, stern, and domineering. This
one could not bring himself to think much of an
Athenian, a chattering people whom Sparta had
reduced to dust. And Xenophon is humble about
it. Spartans are gods, of course, and must rule and
have their way. A little slow of wit, perhaps, but he
does not say so, defers to Cheirisophus in everything, obeys when he is bidden, when he is chidden
admits his error and does better. Only, once in a
while, he permits himself to sweeten this state of
things with pleasant rallying, which passes between the two as it is meant.

A GENTLEMAN OF ATHENS

Still more interesting are such glimpses as we get of Xenophon's handling of the soldiers. Though firm in discipline, it is evident that he treated them as men and fellow citizens. His humanity shows in his repeated efforts to urge on those who would have fallen from fatigue and shows most solidly in the numbers he preserved till the very end. His real democracy shows in his instant response to the man who taunted him with riding when the rest were struggling on foot in a double-quick march. Xenophon at once dismounted and, although in heavy horseman's armor kept up with the foremost until the other soldiers had shamed the taunter back to duty.

This sort of thing proves that he was a born leader of men. His qualities as such came out perhaps even more strongly in holding the troops together and restraining them after they had marched back to safety than when they were in the thickest perils of their progress. How fine was his offer to surrender himself when the Lacedemonian general, Cleander, demanded reparation for an injury! At Byzantium another Lacedemonian officer tricked and betrayed the army, promising them pay and then refusing it. The soldiers forced an entrance into the city, determined to plunder and destroy.

But Xenophon alone stood out squarely against their wrath, showed them the best of reasons for self-restraint, and succeeded in dissuading them. And I repeat, the man who can convey to us these facts about himself and yet leave us with an impression of entire modesty, is surely rare and surely lovable.

The fine passage on leadership in Xenophon's essay on domestic economy gets double significance when we read it as an illustration and a reminiscence of his own splendid achievement: 'Generals differ from one another in this. One sort has followers who shirk both toil and danger and neither approve of obedience nor render it when not absolutely necessary, but are always ready to set themselves up against their commander. The soldiers of such men do not know how to be ashamed when anything disgraceful happens. But really able and excellent and resourceful leaders will take these very same men, sometimes right from the armies of the other sort, and make them ashamed to do anything disgraceful and actually preferring to obey, nay, even rejoicing in obedience, every one of them, and ready to toil with their whole souls, if toiling be called for. And as in individuals there is sometimes a sort of fury of accomplishment, so the whole army of a born leader will long to do something, and the men will vie with each other in performing brave deeds under the captain's eye. Generals who are thus followed are the generals that count, not those that keep their soldiers in good condition, are handy with their own weapons, and have fine horses so that they can lead a charge like a cavalryman. The true general is he who can make men follow him through everything.'

The scene of the 'Anabasis' that lingers longest in the memory of most readers, indeed, the one that is known to many who know nothing of either the 'Anabasis' or its author, is the splendid climax when, after months of struggle and danger, the wanderers toil up a high mountain, and first one and then another and then others and then all join in that splendid and truly Greek outcry, which makes the nerves tingle after two thousand years, '*Thalatta, Thalatta*,' the Sea, the Sea.

Yet to me more than any scene in the 'Anabasis' is the revelation of the heart of the Athenian gentleman who was as good a soldier as he was a writer, and better than either, a lovable man. His finest epitaph is his own sweet description of the elder Cyrus, a great warrior and a great king: 'He was gentle and not without tenderness for human frailty.'

1911

XI
LETTERS OF A ROMAN GENTLEMAN

XI

LETTERS OF A ROMAN GENTLEMAN

To us who dwell in settled peace it is difficult to imagine the violent contrasts that made up the life of the younger Pliny and his contemporaries, and the sudden change from the rule of Domitian — trap-doors under your feet, your best friends suspected, your lightest words twisted — to Nerva's and Trajan's firm, mild, and kindly government, must have been like stepping into heaven from hell.

But Pliny was a man of sunshine under any government. It is most instructive to turn to his picture of his age from that of his somber and indignant contemporaries, Juvenal, Suetonius, Tacitus. Read them and you will think it a wicked world indeed. The great are idle, selfish, cruel, and corrupt. The little are mean, sordid, fawning, debased, contemptible. It is not so with Pliny, who sees and records good in great and little both. So one might easily imagine a double and self-contradicting likeness of our world to-day: on this side, greed, indulgence, godlessness, the rich getting richer, and the poor poorer, one preying and the other hating; on that side, endless acts of kindness and sacrifice, a high ideal and a lowly spirit, love growing everywhere, even where selfishness would hardly let it grow. And both pictures would be true according to the temperament of the artist who drew them.

Not that Pliny entirely overlooks the evils about him. He recognizes that the old world was in some points better: 'Time was when those who wrote in praise of their country were rewarded; but in our age this, like other notable and lovely things, has slipped away.' He shrinks from writing history, 'because, with men as wicked as they are, much more is to be blamed than praised.' Yet, after all, it is wiser to smile than sigh. 'Why am I angry?' he says of the triumphant epitaph of the abominable Pallas. 'It is better to laugh, so that such creatures may not think they have achieved high fortune, when they have made themselves ridiculous.' And he cherishes the noble belief that the best way to make his age worthy is passionately to wish it so: 'I love my generation, praying that it may not be effete and sterile and longing with all my heart that our best citizens may have something fine in their houses besides fine pictures.'

Yet he was a lawyer and so must have known what human nature is. He had a lawyer's training and prejudices, that ingrained love of tradition and precedent which came naturally to Romans, as to Englishmen. Success in a profession so difficult commands his admiration, even when it is accompanied by indifferent honesty, and he cannot but praise the zeal of the unprincipled Regulus whom in other respects he is never weary of abusing. Yet we have his own word for it — and I believe him — that he himself was a shining example of uprightness.

Being a lawyer, he was also an orator, as was essential in that age, however it may be now. He went through all the degrees of that elaborate training which was considered necessary for a great speaker in a time when speech meant so much. What the formal oratory of Pliny may have been we are left to guess, except for one peculiarly artificial and tedious specimen. To us the man is known only through his letters. Yet even these are the letters of an orator. That is, they are not the fresh, simple, spontaneous outpouring of one mind to another, but are arranged, elaborated with a view to literary effect, as if the writer had always a larger audience in mind than the person directly addressed. They are too often clever essays rather than natural correspondence. And Pliny's efforts in this line are the lawful progenitors of a host of frigid things known properly as elegant epistles rather than letters: the productions of Balzac, for instance, or Voiture, or of James Howell, or Pope.

After all, however, the greatest letter writers probably wrote with some self-consciousness. Varied, vivacious, infinitely human as Cicero's letters are, he must have seen posterity out of the corner of his eye. I do not, indeed, suppose that Lamb, even in his later years, for a moment suspected that his careless scribbling would be the delight of English readers all over the world. Or, perhaps, did he? Certainly Cowper did not, nor Edward Fitzgerald. But Madame de Sévigné's letters were read and admired in her lifetime. And she knew it. And could go on discussing her little domestic affairs and her soul with as perfect ease as if she were prattling to you or me by a twilight fire. Horace Walpole, also, divined his future public; and the consciousness sat less lightly on him than on the charming French lady he adored and imitated.

Ease, naturalness, and simplicity are not the characteristics of Pliny. He confesses his methods of procedure in his very first sentence: 'You have often urged me to collect and publish such letters as I have taken a *little extra pains* with.' It recalls

LETTERS OF A ROMAN GENTLEMAN

Horace Walpole at the opening of his epistolary career: 'You have made me a strange request, that I will burn your letters. I make you a still stranger one, that you will keep mine.' Pliny does indeed urge that the style of letters should be simple, *pressus sermo purusque;* but in his case the brevity was always elegantly draped and the refinement that of the drawing-room. Mommsen has justly pointed out that each letter is too often a formal disquisition on one subject; and Joubert, whose exquisite sense of art was never separated from his sense of soul, has judged the Roman letter-writer with unusual severity: 'The younger Pliny took pains with his words. With his thoughts he took no pains.' Pliny himself inadvertently admits much the same thing. After describing minutely to a scientific friend the peculiar behavior of a variable spring, he adds, 'It is your business to examine the causes of such a wonderful phenomenon. My part is simply to put the effect in words.'

Yet, after all, a gift of expression such as Pliny had is no contemptible thing. Much of the best of Shakespeare consists in putting the thoughts of all of us into language of enduring power and charm. And Flaubert, himself the most passionate and human of letter writers, said, '*Il n'y a que les lieux*

*communs et les pays connus pour avoir une intaris-
sable beauté.'* If Pliny could occasionally descend so
low as 'I will make an end of my letter in order that
I may at the same time make an end of the tears
which my letter has called forth,' he could also turn
phrases which must be left untranslated in their
abiding beauty and grace. *'Quod me recordantem
fragilitatis humanæ miseratio subit. Quid enim tam
circumcisum, tam breve quam hominis vita longis-
sima?'* And he could do much more than turn
clever phrases. He could find subtle and apt terms
of literary criticism, he could often convey delicate
and tender emotion, he could describe gayly, if he
chose, or if he chose again, with profound dramatic
effect, as in the swift and telling narrative of the
ghost adventure which befell the philosopher
Athenodorus.

In fact, a man cannot write lengthy letters for
many years without telling us much of value about
his times and about himself. And it is especially to
be noted that, although Pliny was artificial in expression, he had a simple soul. *'Pline, qui est un
naïf,'* says Gaston Boissier, with perfect justice.
And in this Pliny is totally different from Horace
Walpole, who was born sophisticated, with a heart
as wrinkled at twenty as his cheeks at seventy-five.

Walpole tells us exactly what he wishes to tell us and his veracity stands in no proportion to his loquacity. Pliny's soul peeps through every fold of the shimmering drapery in which he would invest it.

For the study of many peculiar characteristics of his age he is of singular interest. For instance, he gives a most effective description of one of those practical philosophers, who, in a sense, anticipated Christianity by doing revival work before vast audiences with a zeal and sincerity that command our admiration. 'There is nothing repugnant in his aspect, nothing dismal, but a lofty gravity. If you met him, you would stand in awe of him, but you would not shrink away. His life is as winning as it is holy. He attacks vices, not men. And does not chastise sinners, but converts them.' In a different vein he depicts those assemblies of friends before which the poets of the day were accustomed to read their productions. Bored! cries Pliny. Why shouldn't they expect to be bored? 'True affection casteth out the fear of boredom, and of what use are your friends anyway if they come together only for their own amusement?' Or he renders, with truly tragic touch, the terrible pathos of a vestal virgin condemned by Domitian to be buried alive for alleged unchastity: 'She was led to her doom, if not innocent, at least with every aspect of innocence. Even when she was stepping down into the vault, her garment caught, and she turned and gathered it up about her: and when the executioner offered her his hand, she drew back, as if to keep her chaste body still pure from the defiling touch.'

Nor are Pliny's letters less fruitful and impressive in anecdotes and sketches of definite historical personages than in the painting of manners in general. Sometimes he adds to the list of terse, pregnant sayings which seem so characteristically Latin and Roman. Every one knows that figure of antique splendor, Arria, who by planting the knife in her own breast encouraged her husband to seek freedom, with the words '*Pæte, non dolet.*' Pliny thinks it an injustice that other sayings of hers as noble should not also be recorded in history — and he records them. Thus to the wife of Scribonianus she cries: 'Do you think I will listen to you, when your husband was killed in your arms and you live?'

More tranquil pictures Pliny has also, of spirits lofty as Arria's, but fruitfully occupied with service to their country, or after years of such service still profitably busying a serene old age. It is refreshing enough to pass from the horrors of Tacitus to the dignified quiet of Spurinna, who lived at peace among his friends and servants, now talking sagely of great deeds done, now reading or writing of the deeds of others, varying these intellectual pursuits with wholesome exercise to keep the temperate body fresh and sound. 'Thus, though he is past his seventy-seventh year, his sight and hearing are perfect, his body agile and alert, and the only trace of old age about him is his wisdom. Such a life is the object of my wish and prayer, and I shall enter upon it whenever the passage of years shall permit me to think of retirement. Meanwhile, I am over-come with a thousand distractions, amid which I comfort myself with the example of this same Spurinna.'

Another noble figure delineated by Pliny is that of his uncle and parent by adoption, Pliny the elder. This distinguished personage, besides being an active and energetic citizen, was an indefatigable student and writer. He wrote extensive histories, of which nothing now survives. He produced also an enormous compilation of myth, tradition, fable, *and* observation, which, under the name of natural history, fed the curiosity of more than a thousand years with things that never happened. It may, however, be justly said of him that 'nothing in his life became him like the leaving of it.' For he perished in a thoroughly scientific attempt to study the great eruption that destroyed Pompeii. After perpetuating forty books of lies, he died of the desire to discover the truth. It was a creditable exit, which the younger Pliny has described in a way to make it more creditable; for the nobility of his uncle's scientific spirit is entirely surpassed by his tranquil acceptance of a terrible situation and his efforts to impart his own tranquillity to others. 'As soon as he appreciated the peril and that escape was unlikely, he began to cheer those about him, to comfort them, to relieve their terrors by gayety or the aspect of gayety. As the long hours dragged on, he beguiled despair by making notes. Then, in the murky and intolerable darkness and horror, he actually slept. Balked in his final attempt to escape by his unwieldy stature and scant breath, and overcome by the smoke and ashes, he was found afterwards, his body entire, unharmed, and clothed as when he had left home; his aspect rather that of the sleeping than of the dead.'

The man Pliny himself is, however, the most interesting thing in his letters; and though he endeavored to show himself only draped, togaed, and in a senatorial attitude, his inmost anatomy is visible enough, if one cares to look for it. We can see him, if we choose, in the rush of his daily business, hurrying about the forum, pleading a cause, attending to a public duty, arranging a little matter for a friend or a great charity for a community, administering a far province, with theaters, and fire departments, and aqueducts, and obstinate Christians to be brought to submission or fed to the wild beasts.

We can see him, much more attractively, in the home life on his great country estates, which the Romans, like the English, loved to cherish, keeping their roots firm in the soil. Pliny himself writes to a friend, of country pleasures: 'I will not say I envy you; but it torments me to think that I cannot have what I long for as the fevered long to bathe in cooling springs. Shall I never break these hampering bonds, since I cannot loose them?'

The Romans, indeed, had not the modern romantic passion for nature. Pliny was no Wordsworth to adore a daffodil or apostrophize a linnet. Such doings would have seemed to him as unworthy as to Socrates. But he loved the country air, and the wide sky, a noble prospect, sparkling sea, and vine-clad hills. 'For a scholar,' as he says of one of his friends, 'a brief acreage suffices, to tread one well-worn path, to know every vine and count every fruit tree.' But he himself is tempted into larger purchasing: 'Change of soil and sky, broad peregrination through one's own possessions, have an infinite charm.' It reminds one of old Burton: 'For peregrination charms our senses with such unspeakable and sweet variety that some count him unhappy that never travelled, a kind of prisoner and pity his case that from his cradle to his old age beholds the same; still, still, still the same.'

And so Pliny gives us a minute and loving picture of his country homes: of Como, where he was born and which he loved with the tenderness of Cowper,

> 'Scenes that soothed
> Or charmed me young, no longer young I find
> Still soothing and of power to charm me still';

of his elaborate and splendid villas in Tuscany and at Laurentum, which he describes with a detail of singular interest to the antiquarian: halls, baths, libraries, porticoes, sitting-rooms for the day and for the night, for company, for privacy; chambers looking out upon the wide prospect, sea or stars, chambers hidden and secluded, 'where no noise of busy people comes, no murmur of the waves, no tumult of the storm, nor glare of lightning, nay, if you wish, not even the light of day, when the shutters are closed'; trim gardens, with flowers, and fruit, and shade; and over the whole dwelling gladsome vines, creeping from roof to roof up to the highest peak of all. They knew what luxury was, these wealthy Romans, and Pliny was by no means one of the wealthiest.

We hear not only of Pliny's abodes, but of his friends, and he was a man to have many of them. The most august was the Emperor Trajan himself, and a collection of letters survives, exchanged between the two when Pliny was governor of the provinces of Bithynia and Pontica. The most interesting of these deal with the treatment of the Christians and show the attitude of a humane and kindly Roman gentleman towards those who, he felt, must be punished, not because they held outlandish beliefs, but because they refused to recognize the supreme control of the civil authority.

Trajan's letters are brief, but courteous and considerate; Pliny's, on the whole, manly and independent. The same thing may perhaps be said of the general tone of the 'Panegyric on Trajan,' Pliny's one remaining piece of oratory. Yet the adulation unavoidable in such a performance will hardly suit an American ear, however it might pass in Berlin or St. Petersburg. 'A religious nation, whose piety has always merited the favor of the immortal gods, can ask nothing further to perfect its happiness than that the gods themselves should imitate Cæsar.' A little strong, is it not? And what interests me most of all is how a person of Trajan's native common sense and practical disposition, not born to this sort of thing, but having grown up a common man among other men, could sit by and listen to it. Was he nauseated? Was he simply bored, enormously? Is it possible that he should have enjoyed it? Did Napoleon?

Pliny had hosts of other friends, not draped in purple. Some of them, many of them, were the first men of the age, whose names echo to us now in a way which would seem to make the mere distinction of their friendship glory enough. Suetonius, Martial — Martial immortalizes Pliny's hospitality and his friend is duly grateful: 'Is it not fitting that I should mourn him who wrote about me thus? He gave me all he had to give. If he had had more, he would have given it. And what can a man give more than praise and glory and eternity?' Tacitus? Tacitus sends his writings for Pliny's revision. Think of it! Revising Tacitus! And Pliny does it. 'I have noted with the utmost care what I think should be altered, what omitted.' What, I wonder?

And Pliny sends his own works for Tacitus's revision in return — which strikes us as a matter of less importance. And he exults in the thought that they two will go down the ages together: 'What a delight that posterity, if it takes heed of us at all, will record everywhere that we lived together in simple faith and brotherly love! A rare and notable thing indeed that two men of nearly equal age and public position, and not unknown in letters (I am forced to speak slightly of you also since I am speaking of myself) should have cherished and fostered one another's studies.' How could he know that in two thousand years Tacitus would be all and he nothing?

Lesser friends he advises also, as to their verses, as to their prose, as to commoner matters still. To one in sickness he sends excellent counsel, with an elaborate account of his own good health and how he got it, which I think can hardly have been very gratifying to the sufferer, any more than Lamb's maliciously delightful epistle to Henry Crabbe Robinson under similar circumstances.

And always Pliny is ready to praise his friends, high and low, as if they were the emperor himself. It reminds one sometimes of Lepidus's ecstasies: His dear Cæsar; but then his dear Antony; Antony, the man of men; but Cæsar is godlike. Pliny was ridiculed, even in his own day, for these excesses, and admits it, and defends himself. 'I confess the fault, I am proud of it. . . . Supposing they are not what I think them. The more fortunate I, since to me they seem so . . . never will you persuade me that I can love my friends too much.' And he lauds the verses of one, the banquets of another, the children of another, till we think we are living in a different and a better world. 'He showed me some letters the other day and said they were his wife's. I thought I was reading Plautus or Terence dissolved in prose. Whether they are his wife's, as he affirms, or his own, as he denies, they do equal credit to the man who can turn out such letters or such a wife.' It is true that in these matters there is a certain tit-for-tatishness; and if Pliny praises, he is not averse to payment in kind. But under all the manner and all the artificial grace, it is, I think, impossible not to recognize genuine love and tenderness: 'You know the weakness of my heart in its affections, you know my anxious fears; and you will not be surprised if I fear most where I hope most.'

One charming phase of Pliny's friendships is his correspondence with illustrious ladies who represent the very best of Roman dignity and Roman virtue. 'There are,' says Professor Dill, 'youths and maidens in the portrait gallery of Pliny whose innocence was guarded by good women as pure and strong as those matrons who nursed the stern, unbending soldiers of the Sabine wars.' To Calvina he writes on matters of business, not omitting to indicate his own probity as well as hers. He advises another friend as to the choice of a tutor for her son: 'From this person your son will learn nothing that will not profit him, nothing that would be better unlearned, and will be reminded no less often than by you or me what ideals he must live up to, what great names are his to sustain.' One should compare also the touching patience and fortitude of a young girl's death: 'She did what the doctors told her, she comforted her father and sister, she kept up her courage even when overcome by weakness. And this endured to the end and was not shaken by the length of her illness or the fear of death.' Other specimens of womanhood there are, to be sure, showing more the influence of prevalent luxury, extravagance, and idleness, as the odd case of that very gay old lady who used the strictest possible care in the education of her grandson, but did not consider it necessary to apply the same methods to herself. 'He lived in the house of his luxurious grandmother after the severest, but also the most submissive fashion. She had a fancy for actors and ran after them rather more than became a lady of her rank. But Quadratus never saw one, on the stage or at home; nor did she wish him to. She told me once, when she was commending her grandson's studiousness, that for herself, to get rid of her wretched feminine leisure, she liked to take a hand in a game or see a play, but when anything of the sort was going on, she bade the boy go to his books, quite as much, I think, out of regard for his innocence as for his learning. You will be astonished at this. So was I.'

As to Pliny's treatment of his slaves we have no evidence but his own, which is remarkably favorable. I am inclined to trust it, however, in default of better. There is, indeed, a curious sentence in the 'Panegyric,' showing how slavery could dull and harden the finer feelings of the kindly and humane. Trajan is extolled because he did not provide immoral and debasing theatrical performances but instead contests 'which inspired the glorious contempt of wounds and death by showing even in *slaves and criminals* the ardor for praise and the thirst for victory.' But numerous passages in the letters indicate a consistent gentleness of treatment, with a desire to secure the welfare of dependents, which makes an agreeable contrast to much that we read of a very different character in other authors. Thus Pliny explains to a friend that he furnished his upper servants with the same wine that he drinks himself. 'Must be rather expensive,' says the friend. 'No,' says Pliny. 'They do not drink what I do. I drink what they do.' His favorite reader falls ill with a hemorrhage. 'How hard it would be for him, what a loss for me, if he to whom all my studies owe their charm should become unfit for study! Who would read my work so well, would cherish it so much? Whose voice would caress my ear like his? But I have hopes that Providence will spare him.' He bewails an excessive mortality among his slaves, but he has at least the comfort of having treated them kindly: 'Two consolations I have, not indeed adequate, but consolations: one, that I allow them to obtain their freedom easily; for those seem not to die too young who have got free; the other, that I allow even the slaves to make a kind of will and that I execute it as such. They devise and enjoin as they wish; and I carry out their wishes. They divide, bestow, and bequeath, provided it is confined to my own household. For the household is, as it were, the country and commonwealth of slaves.'

As regards immediate family, Pliny had no children, though he was twice married. To his second wife, Calpurnia, he writes charming letters, rather literary perhaps in expression, but obviously inspired by genuine feeling. He is glad to hear that she misses him, glad that she reads his verses in his absence. He reads her letters over and over, thinks of her constantly, gives every leisure moment to the thought of her, and is glad to be busy because otherwise he longs for her so much. But the cream of the correspondence in this connection is the letter describing Calpurnia's excellences to her affectionate aunt. No page of Pepys has fuller measure of human nature pressed down and running over: the immense complacent egotism of the husband gauging his wife's perfection by her devotion, the exquisite tact of the wife, playing with deft fingers upon that egotism as upon a many-stopped pipe, guided much by love, no doubt, but also by a fine appreciation of what was for her own comfort and matrimonial ease. 'She has the shrewdest common sense, the most careful housewifery. She loves me as a good wife should. Moreover, her love for me has inspired her with a love for literature. She has all my works, reads them over and over, even learns them by heart. How anxious she is when I am going to speak, how delighted when I have spoken well. She keeps messengers to let her know how I am taking, what applause I get, what the verdict is. When I give a reading, she sits near me, discreetly veiled, and drinks in the praise of me with avid ears. She even sings my verses and sets them to the cither (oh, Mrs. Pepys, oh, Mrs. Pepys!), not taught by art but love, which is the best of masters. For these reasons I feel sure that we shall be happier and happier together as long as we live. For she does not love my youth or my good looks, which fail and fade, but my glory, as behooves one brought up at your hands and taught by your precepts, who, in your dwelling, learned nothing but what was holy and of good report, who even grew to love me under your tutoring.'

From which I conclude that Calpurnia, senior, was a mistress hand in the tutoring of wives. Do you remember Sir Toby's eulogy of Maria? 'She's a beagle, true bred; and one that adores me.' But Sir Toby winked, and Pliny never winks.

By this time it must be evident that our epistolary friend had a good share of amiable vanity. If it were not so amiable, it would certainly be monstrous. And remembering Cicero, I ask myself if many of these world-subduing Romans had a microbe of self-admiration, which would stare us in the face, if we had their letters. Then I think of the exquisite modesty of Virgil, of the fine irony of Horace, of the godlike intellect of Cæsar, which penetrated himself and every one else.

But Pliny had the microbe, if any one ever had. And the art of ingenious — and even entertaining — self-laudation could not be carried further. He sends his works to his friends and asks criticism, with that anxious modesty which we know so well. Be honest. Be sincere. Tell me what you really think. 'I ask it of your confiding simplicity, tell me about my book just what you would tell any one else.' But woe to the simple friend who accepts such an invitation!

Another ingenious device is to repeat to one friend the eulogies of another. 'They say everybody is reading my book, though it came out so long ago; that is, unless the publishers are fooling me.' 'I was very much gratified about my reading. I asked my friends to come if it was convenient and they had nothing else to do. (In Rome there is always something else to do and it is never convenient.) But they came for two days running, and when my modesty was ready to make an end, they insisted on having a third day.'

In his omnivorous appetite for commendation, he admits that he is not too discriminating and even maintains that others are like him. 'All who care for fame and glory enjoy praise even when it comes from their inferiors. . . . Indeed, I don't know why it is, but men prefer their glory broad rather than lofty.'

Written eulogy that comes in the cool quiet of the study is agreeable; but this is nothing compared to the success of the orator, the fury of popular applause, the enthusiasm of the crowd that hangs upon your words, the handshakings and congratulations that come after. 'My turn arrives. I rise . . . O wonderful! Those who were but now against me receive every word with attention and applause. I conclude. Veiento tries to reply. Nobody will listen. . . . There was hardly a man in the Senate who did not embrace me, did not kiss me, did not overwhelm me with praise.' It recalls — afar off — that most wonderful scene of Mr. Pepys's great speech and the climax of commendations which agitated his spirit with delight: 'From thence I went to Westminster Hall, where I met Mr. G. Montagu, who came to me and kissed me, and told me that he had often heretofore kissed my hands, but now he would kiss my lips: protesting that I was another Cicero, and said all the world said the same of me. Mr. Ashburnham, and every creature I met there of the Parliament, or that knew anything of the Parliament's actings, did salute me with this honor: — Mr. Godolphin: — Mr. Sands, who swore he would go twenty miles, at any time, to hear the like again, and that he never saw so many sit four hours together to hear any man in his life, as there did to hear me; Mr. Chichly, — Sir John Duncomb, — and everybody do say that the kingdom will ring of my abilities, and that I have done myself right for my whole life; and so Captain Cocke, and others of my friends, say that no man had ever such an opportunity of making his abilities known; and, that I may cite all at once, Mr. Lieutenant of the Tower did tell me that Mr. Vaughan did protest to him, and in his hearing it, said so to the Duke of Albermarle, and afterwards to W. Coventry, that he had sat twenty-six years in Parliament and never heard such a speech there before: for which the Lord God make me thankful! and that I may make use of it, not to pride and vainglory, but that, now I have this esteem, I may do nothing that may lessen it!'

Delightful as this contemporary approbation is,

however, Pliny is insatiably looking forward. Posterity, years upon years upon years, must honor him, or he will not be satisfied: 'Whether they are right or wrong in praising me I do not know; but my one prayer is that posterity may be right or wrong in the same way.' And, with good critical tact, he begs for a scrap of the immortality which Tacitus can bestow: 'I know I am right in predicting that your history will be immortal. For that reason I frankly confess that I should be glad to be mentioned in it.' Alas, he may have been, but not in that portion that has endured.

We smile at this vanity of Pliny's. Who could help it? But, as I have said, it is amiable, and, as has been long ago remarked, vanity is often associated with excellent qualities. The fine, the really beautiful expressions of moral, almost Christian feeling, which occur in the letters, are not merely expressions; and when we read, 'I call him most perfect who himself forgives others as if he were daily liable to fall and refrains from falling as if there were no forgiveness,' we are safe in assuming that the writer practiced his own precept, as far as frail human nature may. He does, indeed, beg pardon for writing verses that are too gamesome; but probably it was because he thought, with others since, that in poetry to be gamesome was to be great; and I imagine that his verses were no more like the verses of Martial than the letters of Martial would have been like the letters of Pliny.

Kindly he certainly was and practically benefi-cent, though even here his failing haunts him and he informs us of his charities in ample phraseology, at the same time remarking that 'those who adorn their good deeds with fine words seem not to be telling because they have done, but to have done in order that they might be telling.' Telling or not, however, he did the deeds, built temples, founded schools, had a friendly word for trouble and an open hand for suffering, in short, lived the life of a useful citizen and an honorable gentleman, if not, as he would have wished, that of a great poet and an im-mortal genius.

It is to be noted, also, that Pliny's essential vir-tue does not proceed from any especially religious motive, as does, for instance, that of the Athenian gentleman who in some ways resembles him, Xeno-phon. With Xenophon the gods are daily, nightly present. He considers them in his getting up and in his lying down. To do wrong is to offend them and risk their anger. To do right is always pleas-ing and acceptable to them. Now Pliny is by no means directly irreligious. Indeed, a strong tincture of superstition appears in him, as in so many of his contemporaries — witness the excellent ghost story that he tells with positive assurance as to the facts and much credulity as to the causes. But skepticism was too deeply rooted in a Roman of that day for the divine to be often recognized as a spring of daily action, and Pliny rarely, if ever, refers to it as such. His goodness, his kindliness, are native, instinctive, spring from pure human love and charity, and are surely none the less creditable to him on that account.

And thus, as we read him here in far-off America, he has an undying glory, as undying glories go. Only it is not for his verses, but for his virtues. Would that have satisfied him? I fear not. Long since it was remarked that we had rather be praised for the head than for the heart. And yet it is something to be remembered for two thousand years as one who was a little better than the average.

1912

XII
OVID AMONG THE GOTHS

XII

OVID AMONG THE GOTHS

THE haphazard pun by which Touchstone compares himself among his goats to the honest poet Ovid among the Goths has a double infelicity, because Ovid was not among the Goths and because he is ill-described by 'honest' in the parliamentary sense in which Touchstone employs the word. Nevertheless, the familiar reference will serve to introduce the most pitiable figure in all classic literature, who has made himself interesting by the minute, if monotonous, description of his woes. *Cano tristia tristis.* My song is dismal because I am. As he had sung lovers without loving, gods without believing, and heroes, though perfectly incapable of heroism, some of us prefer his dismal strains to anything else he wrote.

Boissier, with unusual exaggeration, declares his belief that Ovid, before his exile, was the happiest man that ever existed. This would be a rash assertion, even about men whom we know far better. But it is clear that Ovid's early life must have been a peculiarly fortunate one. Born just at the beginning of the Augustan age, he had none of the personal recollection of preceding horrors which gave gravity to Virgil and Horace; yet he knew by hearsay enough to impart a sharper zest to the pleasures of peace and luxury and ease. Placed in a comfortable social position and financially well-to-do, he had friends in the literary and in the fashionable sets both. At that time the whole Roman world was mad for pleasure. The men were excluded from politics and had nothing to do but run after the women. The women were restless, idle, and eager for the admiration of the men. Banquets, theaters, shows, public readings — every diversion which would bring the sexes into social contact was sought for with incessant eagerness.

In short, Cupid was the reigning deity. Marrying, giving in marriage — and forgiving in marriage — have rarely been carried on more hilariously. Ovid himself was married thrice; but this was moderation. His claims to popularity were quite different. Of all that carnival of amorous gayety, legitimate and illegitimate, he was the poet and high-priest. It is true that genuine love requires little literary stimulus. 'A lady asked me the other day,' says Anatole France, 'of what use were poets. I told her they helped us to love, but she assured me one could love very well without them.' Ovid him-

316

self acknowledges the same thing with charming candor: 'My verses teach only what everybody knows already.' Nevertheless, gaudy youth will always, with the hero of Shakespeare, like books that are well-bound and that treat of love. And Ovid, inexhaustible in poetic ingenuity, fed the popular appetite, first with a glowing account of his own experiences, and then with an elaborate treatise on the Art of Love, which proved him at once to be an expert, and no doubt won him the applause and admiration of all who had been, were, or wished to be successful lovers.

Few men were better able to enjoy or appreciate such a position. He had not sufficient depth of nature for profound sympathy, but he was eminently mobile, sensitive, and quick to respond to outside influences. He was a thorough egotist, but he had also the strong social instinct which obscures egotism when it cannot obliterate it. He was selfish, yet he was kindly where it cost him nothing, and though he was intensely ambitious, Landor has well pointed out that few poets have spoken of their contemporaries with less jealousy than he. In all his vast work, there is little trace of genuine passion, and consequently his poetry lacks the high note that passion gives. He is fanciful rather than imaginative, gay rather than merry, ingenious rather than profound. In fact, ingenuity haunts him everywhere. A professional story-teller, he can never lose himself in his story, as do Boccaccio and Chaucer, Dumas and Scott. The whole world to him, earth, heaven, and hell, is matter for perpetual cleverness. He reminds one often of Oscar Wilde, and, like Wilde, he seemed of all men least fitted to bear the sudden blast of misery that came upon him.

For, in the height of his popularity, when he was doing his best and soberest work, when all Rome admired and applauded him, he was sent by the Emperor Augustus into perpetual exile at the end of the world. The exact, immediate cause of this misfortune is not clearly known. Ovid refers to it often, but in veiled language and with obscure hints only. The most probable conjecture is that he was in some way involved in one of the scandals of the imperial family and had seen and heard more than he should have done. Back of this pretext, however, it seems evident that the emperor wished to punish the poet for his very objectionable verses. Among other ambitions Augustus had that of desiring to be a reformer. He found Rome brick and left it marble. He also found it corrupt and wished to leave it virtuous. This was a good deal more difficult. No coadjutors, he thought, would be more helpful than the poets. Virgil, and even Horace, fell in with the revival policy admirably. But Ovid, Ovid — he triumphed with ecstasy in everything the emperor most wished to suppress. Therefore, when a good occasion presented itself, he had to suffer.

He did suffer. At the age of fifty he was exiled to Tomi, a little colony, half Greek, half barbarian, on the Black Sea, near the mouth of the Danube. The decree came upon him suddenly and he gives a piteous description of his hurried departure, the scanty preparation, the forlorn leavetakings. A rough and violent winter voyage brought him, after many narrow escapes, to the dreary, barren edge of civilization, where he was to spend eight miserable years, and from which he sent forth one prolonged wail of metrical agony. 'To think that one whose name was a household word in Rome should have to live among the Bessi and the Getes!' That is the perpetual note.

Could there be a more curious psychological study than such a man, thrown into such surroundings and himself supplying careful notes on his sufferings and experiences? For, in his long series of verse letters to home friends, he details, with cruel

monotony, if not the incidents, at least the emotions of his daily life. As might have been expected,
with his character, disaster so complete brings
complete moral collapse. 'If you met me in the
street, you would not know me,' he writes to one
friend; 'my prime of life is so overcome with ruin.'
He does, indeed, occasionally pride himself on bearing up with courage. 'My soul is equal to my evils.
From that my body gets strength and bears things
not to be borne.' Again, 'All woes come upon me.
But my soul bears all woes and gives my body
strength to bear them.' These are vague flashes,
however. As a general thing, he finds no consolation, no comfort, no refuge.

There seems to be little effort to seek for charm
or interest in his surroundings, yet some charm or
interest they must have had, surely. All through
his earlier work there are constant traces of delight
in the beauty of nature, and though his expression
of this is too apt to be deformed by the attempt at
cleverness, it has often exquisite feeling.

> *'Nec minimum refert, intacta rosaria primus,*
> *An sera carpas paene relicta manu.'*

To be sure, the nature of the Scythian steppes was
far remote from that of Tibur or Pæstum; yet
one would think its breadth, its color, its vastness,

must have made some spiritual appeal. To Ovid there is none, nothing but barrenness, shuddering desolation, horror, and cold, cold, forever cold. It is most curious to note how again and again he starts to paint what he sees about him, and, before he knows it, slips into painting what he does not see; violets, roses, the breath of vineyards, merry barefoot maidens dancing in the autumn sun. His heart aches as he remembers, and his light verses grow heavy with the weight of tears.

There is one natural solace that he would indulge in, if he could, and his longing for it is a great element of attraction in him. Apparently even in the giddy days of laughter and vanity, he had learned, or had not forgotten, the true Roman love of the soil. He recalls with sadness those gardens — tended now by whom? — which he himself was wont to cherish, and the trees he planted from which others must pluck the fruit. The touch of the soil, he feels, would make him forget thought, the homely contact of goats or sheep. He would like to learn the Getic cries for guiding oxen, to grasp the plough in his hand and cast the seed upon the turned earth. His quick imagination fires with the idea — these fields, why not clear the tangled weeds out of them? Why not bring water to the parched and sterile soil? Yet, after all, what is the use? This is not civilized Italy. And what profits labor, when the marauding Scythian may sweep away a season's effort in one night?

But, if nature is inadequate and uncertain, there are still men, and women, and children. Surely they ought to be all the more interesting because they are different from those at home. We are told that Ovid was the keenest of observers. Always 'in the closest contact with human nature,' says Sellar; and Landor, 'that poet who with all his levity has more unobtrusively sage verses than any, be he Roman or Athenian.' It may be so; but he appears to find very little worth his talent in an eight years' residence at Tomi. Rare indeed is any touch of genuine observation: 'The women pound corn, instead of spinning, and carry heavy vessels of water on their bent heads.' Occasionally he sketches in broad outlines the hurrying throng as he sees it about him: 'You want to know something of these people of Tomi where I dwell? A mixed company, between Greek and Getic, but more of the half-subdued Getic than the Greek. . . . Not one of them who does not carry quiver and bow and arrows dark with viper's gall. Fierce voices, cruel faces, the true breed of Mars, unshorn, unshaven, quick to strike with the knife that every man of them carries at his thigh. Among these creatures, dear friend, now dwells thy poet, alas, forgetful of his dainty loves; such things he hears and such he sees.' And the shudder of his rising hair and nerve-racked flesh makes his verses harsh as the filing of a saw:

> '*Nec vacat, in qua sint positi regione Tomitæ,*
> *Quaerere, finitimo vix loca nota Getæ;*
> *Aut quid Sauromatæ faciant, quid Iazyges acres,*
> *Cultaque Oresteæ Taurica terra deæ.*'

If he had not leisure even to observe or describe the human movement that was going on about him, it is hardly to be supposed that he would enter into it with sympathy, that he would make acquaintances or friends, and find in new affection, however different, some recompense for the loss of the old. Apparently he did not. 'Here is no friend,' he says, 'whose chat can wile away the slowly slipping hours.' And in a moment of petulance he brands everybody with savage condemnation — 'The men are hardly worthy of the name: the wolves are only a little more savage.' It is true that when his neighbors at last find out this attitude and not unnaturally take offense at it, he apologizes. No, no, not you, he says, I never quarreled with you. It is my own situation I grieve over here. You are all kind to me, very, very kind. It is your country I don't like. And you don't like it yourselves. With time he overcomes his prejudices, learns the native language, writes in it, is praised and honored, and finds, no doubt, a certain satisfaction in being so.

Yet, even allowing for all the circumstances, the man's bearing seems to me thoroughly consistent with what we know of him. He was quick and sensitive. He had no depth of kindliness or sympathy. It is only necessary to place the elaborate love letters of his heroines beside Dante's Francesca or Virgil's Dido to perceive this. But compare Ovid with a much lesser personage than Dante or Virgil, with Dumas père, whom in some ways he resembles. Dumas would have felt such an exile from Paris as keenly as Ovid; but in three months he would have had three love affairs, have hobnobbed with Greek and Sarmate, have rigged a stage and put on melodramas that would have drawn tears and coin from every Getic soul. Since he could not go to Rome, he would have brought Rome to Tomi, and the present applause of the barbarians would almost have made up for remote Roman forgetfulness.

I ask myself, further, whether adversity accomplished any change in Ovid's inner life, whether the loss of all he loved brought the least profit in self-examination, in stiffening of spiritual fiber, in purifying and elevating of moral tone. The response is slighter than one could wish. Of repentance for early folly and indiscretion, real regret for having offended, not only against the wishes of Augustus, but against all the purer and finer traditions of Roman morals, there is hardly a trace. Once or twice, indeed, the poet's agony wrings from him what sounds like a cry of genuine remorse. 'When I was fortunate and happy, I toyed with youthful, happy things. Now at last I come to regret it.' Again, even more earnestly: 'Oh, I repent, I repent, if ever wretchedness is to be trusted; and my error wrings my soul. My fault is worse to me than my exile and to have sinned is worse than to suffer the penalty. So help me God, to whom that sin is known, the penalty may be removed, the sin will last forever.' It seems hard not to believe such a fervor of confession as this. Yet with Ovid one never knows. His general tone in regard to his shortcomings is much more one of apology and of defense. Others have done far worse than he. Look at the old poets, Greek and Latin. What things are written there and no poet was ever exiled for them! Look at the

stage — a horror, beside which his verses are innocent. And there is the old plea, that he gave the
public only what it asked for. Altogether, it seems
as if the regret were less for having offended morals
than for having offended Augustus.

Also, misery should have bred tenderness and
tolerance as well as repentance. Did it? I have already noted Landor's stress upon Ovid's general
kindliness. 'I wish well to Ovidius, for he speaks
well of everybody,' says Messala, in his charming
dialogue with Tibullus. This is in the main un-
deniable, and sometimes a deeper spirit of forgiveness breathes in the melancholy elegies: 'Your
loyalty is precious. As for those who turned their
backs and fled with fortune, let us forgive them.'
Yet over against this we must set that curious outburst of rage called 'Ibis,' in which the poet hurls
his whole arsenal of fury against an enemy who
persists in hounding him even in his exile. Such a
luxury of cursing, such a finished, ornate, elaborate
triumph of anathema can hardly be produced elsewhere outside the ecclesiastical perfection of Doctor Slop. A mere literary exercise, in imitation of
Callimachus, say some. Literary the thing is, to the
point of frigidity, like much of Ovid's writing.
But literary or not, a mind which could occupy

itself with such vindictiveness can hardly be said to have been chastened, or sweetened, or purified by adversity.

The truth is, during the whole long eight years, the exile thought of but one thing, getting home again. This effort sustained him, this hope comforted him. Without it his only refuge would have been the suicide from which a faithful friend saved him when the blow first fell.

From the beginning he keeps up a perpetual epistolary bombardment upon every one in Rome who is likely to have interest or influence. The emperor, of course, stands first and to him Ovid addresses appeal after appeal, varying his petitions with all possible ingenuity of flattery. The longest of these letters is the elaborate defense referred to above, in which the poet justifies his errors by the example of others. It would seem as if nothing could have shown more lack of judgment. If Augustus was really bent on reforming the world, he was not likely to be gratified by the argument that all literature was against him. A sincere offer of assistance would probably have gone further; but no doubt he knew that of this Ovid was quite incapable. At any rate, neither argument, nor gross flattery, nor piteous plea made any impression, unless Ovid was right in imagining that the emperor was preparing to reconsider at the time of his death.

Below the throne there was a long list of friends and acquaintances to whom Ovid writes with agonized entreaty. What their response was we can only guess; but it is likely to have implied more or less amiable evasion. In the first series of his letters, the 'Tristia,' he mentions few names, appealing now to one great personage, now to another, anonymously, with the evident fear that they would not wish to be compromised. But in the 'Pontic Epistles' he drops this precaution, whether because he has grown hopeless or because the whole story has become too public for comment to be dangerous. Among his correspondents are some of the greatest names of Rome and he addresses them in every variety of tone. Now he learns of one, trusted utterly, who has betrayed him, and it seems as if the foundations of his universe were shaken. Or again, a mere acquaintance, from whom he expected nothing, proves loyal, and his heart exults with hope. In his extremity, he even goes outside the limits of Roman friendship and appeals to the barbarian king Cotys, if by any chance his influence may avail with the imperial autocrat. Sometimes he reproaches bitterly, for real or imagined neglect:

'The ants never throng to a deserted granary. Lose your wealth and you will lose your friends.' Sometimes he declares that he will give up the attempt, reconcile himself, forget: 'There are wounds that are made worse by meddling with them. It is better to let them alone.' But this mood does not last. No diversion, no reaction lasts; all give place, and that speedily, to the prolonged, renewed, inevitable wail: Rome, Rome, bring me back to Rome, or if not that, get me delivered from this Scythian horror, this bleak and frigid epitome of hell.

There is one intercessor in whom the poet places more confidence than in any other — his wife; and his letters to her are the most curious of all. How genuine was his affection for her? She was his third matrimonial experiment, and we have no means of knowing how deep his conjugal devotion may have been before disaster came. Certainly, to hear him, you would think they must have been a pair of doves. She is the half of his soul. He would be glad indeed to perish if only she can be safe. Her agony at his departure — so he says — was indescribable: swooning, torn hair, gelid limbs, a first impulse to go with him, a second to die since she cannot have him, the third to live only with the sacred purpose of devoting herself to his recall.

From the far shores of Scythia he writes back, commending her fidelity. He knows all she is doing for him. She is as chaste as Penelope, as faithful as Laodamia, and he wraps her in the purple garment of mythology which he had ready-made for all the numerous and varied ladies whom it served his turn to celebrate. Her birthday comes. He will honor it in frozen Tomi as he used to in Italian sunshine. 'Blessed festival, come hither, hither to my far-off dwelling-place; come all bright and shining, alas, too much unlike my own.'

Yet there grows later a little impatience, if you are watching carefully. Why can't she do something? The years are going, going. There is the empress. Surely she can appeal to her. Risk? What if there is a little risk? Even if she loses her life in the attempt, there was a king Admetus who had a queen, Alcestis. But there — bore my wife, so faithful, though a little timid, a little inexperienced in the world's wicked ways? I am not the sort of man for that. And one asks one's self, What was she doing all those years? Really longing, loving; or betraying, forgetting? Who may know?

Whatever doubt may attach to Ovid's affection for his wife, none attends the brief glimpse we get of his daughter, the lovely-named Perilla, who had probably little influence and apparently much charm. He makes a tender reference to her in the 'Fasti': 'One daughter I have, and may she long outlive me. With her alive I cannot but be happy.' And one letter he writes to her from his melancholy exile. It is sad enough, but it has singularly winning grace. Where will it find her, he wonders, sitting with her gentle mother, or busy with her books? Wherever she may be, he knows she will snatch it eagerly, wild with desire to know how he is and what he is about. Those books — does she remember how they enjoyed them together, made verses together, each helped the other in the lovely converse of the Muses? Those books — let her cling to them still. She need not fear that song will be her ruin as it has been his. For she can sing nothing but what is innocent and pure. And her beauty will fade, and age with noiseless foot will come stealing upon her; but the delight of thought and the enchanting grace of poetry can never grow old.

So this vision of fresh girlhood breaks in, like a gleam of sunshine, on the varied monotony of complaint. But the clouds close again at once, and if the poet thinks of anything but his woes, he does not speak of it. Long day after long day he broods on misery. Ill health? No, not ill health, at least not always. He has been frail from childhood, but on the whole he bears his troubles physically well. Perhaps the strong fresh air even invigorates nerves spent with too much Roman luxury. But for the mind — what is there to hope? Days of terror, years of remorseless, cold life unrelieved by affection, or society, or glory; and death — death in that barren desert, untended, unpitied, unbewailed. Why, if tales be true, his Roman ghost must wander forever among Sarmatic shadows. Ah, no, rather perish on the pyre, body and soul. But at least he begs that those who love him — if any love him — may bring back his ashes in a little urn, that so he may not be an exile even after death.

From thoughts bitter as these, memory, though also bitter, affords a sort of refuge, and the poet lives much in the past, forgetting in the pale glow of his imagination the wastes of Scythia and the battle cries of Gete and Sarmate. Rome hangs ever before him, Rome so immeasurably the greatest thing in the Roman world. Paris to a Frenchman means much. Perhaps no Parisian could be permanently happy away from it. Still, there are other capitals besides Paris. And some flavor of civilization would be found in almost any modern exile.

OVID AMONG THE GOTHS

To a Roman, outside of Rome there was nothing —
not even in Athens or the gorgeous cities of the
East. Thus it is that Ovid tells over to himself all
those past days and the delights of them, visits
again known streets and squares, basks in sunlit
porticos, hears the common cries that once seemed
harsh and now reëcho so deliciously.

Not the city only, but the things that were done
there, fill his memory and sting it with a terrible,
enchanting pain. Youth, youth is fled far enough
anyway, but how much farther it seems, and dim-
mer, and sweeter, across those stern and savage
seas. Now he recalls pleasant days and merry
companions: 'I remember so well our pastimes together and the dainty jests that sped the moments
swiftly. The hours seemed too brief for the interchange of thought and the day was gone sooner
than what I had to tell you.' Now he goes over,
less, no doubt, for his correspondent than for himself, a rapid sketch of his childhood and young manhood, touches tenderly the memory of his lost brother, dwells at length on his passion for study and
poetry and the friends it brought him. Virgil he saw,
Horace he heard, Propertius he knew well. Where
are they now? Or his mind turns to earlier wander-
ings, far, far different from those he has lately

known. Then, with his friend Macer, he visited the purple East, Greece, and Sicily — all sunshine, all gayety, all charm. It is one thing to travel at your own wayward will, in jovial company, when pleasant sights suggest quick thoughts, and quick thoughts breed harmless jests, and when above all, if you choose, you can turn your ship's prow backward and in a few hours be in Rome again. But Scythia!

And those who have dreamed dreams of loved ones lost and joy vanished will know what dreams must have been to Ovid. To see, to hear, actually to touch, and then to have all snatched away again in a moment! 'My dreams affright me with the shadow of real things and my inner sense wakes ever for my ruin. Sometimes I seem to shun the flying arrows and to extend my captive hands for cruel chains. Or again, fooled by the treachery of too sweet sleep, I behold the far dwellings of my own country, and speak my fill with the friends I love and with my darling wife. Then I awake, and see how false was my delight, and my present state is made worse by the keen perception of all that I have lost. Thus, whether day beholds this wretched head, or whether the dewy steeds of night are passing slowly, my heart is melted within me by perpetual care, even as new wax is melted by a sudden flame.'

334

And love? What of love? He had been the poet of love, the prophet of love, the high-priest of love. Will love desert him now? The memory of past triumphs and successes still lingers with him — a torture, or a delight? Cupid appears to him in a dream and comforts him with the near prospect of release from exile. Again, in a more melancholy moment, he composes his epitaph and calls upon all true lovers to pray for his repose. Yet I hardly think love, as a personal emotion, can ever have been a very important element in his life. At any rate, when he arrived at Tomi, he was well past middle age, and there is certainly no indication of amatory solace during his sojourn there. I have said that Dumas would have had many love-affairs upon his hands. But Ovid was of a different temper. He himself tells us that he never gave a thought to such things and naïvely confirms the assertion by declaring that his surroundings afforded no opportunity. It seems more than probable that he is another striking instance of a fact singularly attested in the correspondence of Sterne, that the men who have written most freely on sexual matters are, for obvious reasons, apt to be personally of a rather frigid temperament.

No, I imagine that the recollection of love and

all his dealings with it and all it had done — or undone — for him, afforded Ovid little but bitterness. And though he would have comprehended but imperfectly the beautiful sentences of his great admirer Landor, he would have been quite ready to subscribe to them: 'Before I left Ovidius when I returned his visit, he read to me the commencement of some amatory pieces, at which, if I smiled, it was in courtesy, not approbation. From the mysteries of religion the veil is seldom to be drawn, from the mysteries of love never. For this offense the gods take away from us our freshness of heart and our susceptibility of pure delight.'

One consolation Ovid had in his misery, however, one serious, high, enduring consolation, without which it is difficult indeed to see how he could have survived; and that was literature. All his life he was essentially a literary man. It was not only that he loved glory, as Lucretius and Virgil did. It was not only that he had an exquisite delight in artistic expression, as Horace had. It was more than that. He looked at all life, at nature, at religion, at man and woman, at himself, from the literary point of view, as much as ever Flaubert or D'Annunzio. Through all his emotions, through all his experiences, you trace that curious detachment, that double personality, by which the born writer at once lives, and stands by and watches himself live. He had the writer's love of finish, the writer's vanity, the writer's pretense of belittling his work when it is all on earth he cares for. How admirable is his declaration in one line that he has burned his great poem, with the confession in the next that it is safely extant in other copies!

The excess of this literary preoccupation accounts, I think, for the defects of even Ovid's best poetry. He never loses himself in his subject, is never lifted up, nor swept away. Sellar is impressed with the poet's freshness of imaginative sympathy, and the Countess Martinengo-Cesaresco feels that he approaches the old myths with the buoyancy and impressionability of a child. But Boissier calls him a poet of fashion, a parlor poet, and I do not see how any one can read him widely without agreeing with Boissier. He had, it is true, immense fertility of invention, an extraordinary richness and breadth of fancy. But always at critical moments there comes the false note, the sense of artifice, the intrusion of the writer's cleverness between the reader and the thing portrayed. Light, color, swiftness, ease, gayety, are always there; but human truth is not there. Even in Ovid's lamentations, the sincerest things he ever wrote, this literary ingenuity is often near at hand. A sob turns to an epigram and a bitter memory is dissolved in a mythological catalogue.

Yet the fact remains that literature was his comfort, his solace, his delight, a pale delight, and sometimes chilled by the frozen winds of Scythia, but at least something to turn to, to banish thought and sweeten care. He is a worker, has always been a worker he tells us, and even in exile and misery he works. On the voyage out, when the high seas are wetting his manuscript, he is making verses. After years of absence, in the midst of barbarians, and with hostile uproar sounding in his ears, he is making verses still. Sometimes his patience fails, sometimes he loses his temper even with the Muse, his best, most faithful, only friend; after all, she misled him, she ruined him. But it does not last long. She is a mistress whose sovereign charm no lover can resist, and he returns to her with a cry which all her followers will echo and cherish: 'As the wounded votary of Bacchus does not feel her wounds, when sense is numbed by the wild revel in Idæan woods, so when my heart is touched by that thyrsus, ever green, the spirit within me rises above all human ills. It forgets exile, forgets the frigid barriers of the Scythian sea, forgets even the anger of the gods. I might have drunk the cup of Lethe, breeder of sleep, so free is my soul from the bitter contact of adversity.

Nor is it merely as diversion, distraction, minister of forgetfulness, that the Muse helps lonely sorrow such as Ovid's was. There is something in the outcry, too, something of relief and comfort in proclaiming one's woes in imperishable beauty which distant ears will hear, if ears at hand do not. Strange, that those things we would not, could not, utter in close confidence to a near friend, we are ready to pour out from the housetops that whoso will may profit by them. And thus, no doubt, Ovid, like Leopardi, like Byron, like Heine, found consolation in embalming his griefs in what he fondly hoped might be eternal verses.

One thing is curious. The sufferings Ovid sang were real, tangible, indisputable, such as no one could doubt or laugh at. Byron's, on the other hand, were for the most part subjective, willful, matter of the mind not of the body. Yet, perhaps from this very fact, Byron's seem to us far more noble, more worthy, more dignified. Neither was thoroughly manly, but of the two Byron was very much more so.

Manly or not, however, Ovid succeeded in making millions of posterity think about him. The assurance of this would have been some slight alleviation of his misery. And indeed there were times when, with the splendid prophetic vision of a great poet, he needed no external assurance. Thus the closing lines of the charming letter to his daughter are among the finest, not only of Ovid, but of any Roman poet: 'Even I, though I lack fatherland and love and home, though all things have been taken from me that can be taken, yet I have with me my genius as an eternal joy. Over that even Cæsar has no power. Whoever wills may end my mortal life. But my fame will live on when I have passed away. So long as martial Rome, victorious upon her seven hills, shall sway the orbed world, so long mankind shall read my verses.' Moments like that must have paid for some days even of exile.

1913

XIII
PORTRAIT OF A SAINT

XIII

PORTRAIT OF A SAINT

FRANCIS OF SALES was a man who, of his own choice, gave up all the good things of this world out of pure love for the kingdom of God. Born in 1567, the eldest son of a rich and noble French family, with every career of arms or state open to him, he chose the church, and without the use of political influence, or intrigue, simply by purity, devotion, and a charming power over souls, became a bishop infinitely beloved, and was duly canonized after his death. Few have better deserved sainthood.

The life of Saint Francis has been obscured by numerous hagiographers with the pious incense of spiritual legend. But one disciple, Camus, Bishop of Belley, has left us a study, 'L'Esprit de Saint François de Sales,' which portrays the saint in his daily life almost with the patience and fidelity of a Boswell. Indeed, in some respects, Boswell is outdone; for Camus tells us that when his idol visited him, in order to get more exact material for his record, he bored a hole through into Francis's room, and watched his actions even when he thought himself alone. This is an extreme biographical

343

solicitude to which I do not read that Dr. Johnson was subjected. Perhaps he would not have come out quite so well as Saint Francis is reported to have done.

But far more valuable than such gossipy external observation is Saint Francis' own writing, his numerous sermons and treatises, and the intimate personal letters of which a vast number have been preserved.

First, for the shadows, such as they are. It was a bitter time. The battles of the Reformation were fighting everywhere, and both sides were tempted to resort to words and deeds that our cooler — and less believing — age can hardly tolerate. Francis, as bishop in the neighborhood of Protestant Geneva, was drawn into some actions and more words that we are very far from approving. But everything shows that, for his time, he was mild and tolerant, and really cherished the spirit of his own beautiful sentence, written in later life: 'He who preaches with love preaches enough against the heretics, though he does not utter one word of controversy.'

In dealing with these practical sides of the divine calling, Sainte-Beuve justly points out that Francis shows the business instincts of a man of the world.

PORTRAIT OF A SAINT

He was no recluse, no shy and quiet scholar. He could mingle with men, and influence them, and guide them in everyday pursuits. He even complains of the distraction this brought upon him. 'The affairs of this diocese are not streams but torrents.' When he was sent to Paris for things semipolitical, semi-religious, he so demeaned himself that Henri Quatre, that supreme man of the world, spoke of him and treated him with as much affection as respect. If necessary, he could recall high persons to their duty with prophetic sternness, as when he reminded the Duke of Savoy that princes were bound to give great thought to great measures, 'on pain of eternal damnation.'

It must not be supposed, however, that he was one of the busy, meddling prelates who long to arrange matters of this world as well as of the other. On the contrary, I have sought far for even subtle and indirect evidence of such ambition and have found none. He went into the world for duty. For delight he gladly and often went out of it.

In other words, he was preëminently a man of the spirit, a man to whom God meant everything. Not that he was a great theologian. He read widely, read the Fathers thoroughly. His own treatise, 'On the Love of God,' contains much subtle theological discussion, which some may find of profit; but he is always glad to break away from difficult problems and the vain effort to search out the unsearchable. 'Poor little insect,' he says to his own understanding, 'poor little insect, bred from the corruption of my flesh, why will you scorch your wings at this immense fire of divine omnipotence, which would consume and devour the seraphim, if they thrust themselves into such expense of curiosity? No, poor butterfly, thy business is to be lost in adoration, and not to dangle thy plummet in the deep.'

This is the mystic's self-abandonment. Saint Francis took to it far more kindly than to the debates of Augustine and Aquinas. The treatise above mentioned is full of mystical ecstasy, drenched with it, and Francis' letters contain many passages even more significant in their high-wrought rapture and their absolute submission to the will of God. 'Keeping my soul forever in His divine presence, with a joy not over-impetuous, but, as it seems to me, rich enough to express a perfect love to Him; for nothing in this world is worth our love; it should be all for that Saviour who has given us all of His.'

But the essential characteristic of Saint Francis'

religion was neither theology nor ecstasy, but sunshine. His heart was simple, and to the simple is
given the supreme heritage of joy. He did not, indeed, wholly claim this for himself. 'I am, to be
sure, by no means simple, but I love simplicity
with an extraordinary love.' He was simpler than
he thought, and pure, and straightforward, and
direct.

He was humble, also, did not exalt himself even
by the assumption of humility. 'Humility, simplicity of heart and of affection, and spiritual submission, are the solid foundations of the religious
life.' So he wrote, so he thought, and his practice
bore out the letter of his teaching.

Above all, in his simplicity and in his humility, he
had charm. The adjective that occurs most frequently in his writings, that occurs with a singular,
penetrating, impressive repetition, is *suave*, which
we must free from all its English associations of in-
sincerity and keep only in its primitive significance,
of grace, gentleness, sweetness, tenderness. 'Let us
be saved with our amiable relative, Saint Francis
of Sales,' writes Madame de Sévigné. 'He leads
people to Paradise by a pleasanter road than the
gentlemen of Port Royal.' And one of the great
controversialists of the Reformation indicated

admirably the same thing: 'If it is only a question of convincing, I can do it; but if you want to convert men, take them to the Bishop of Geneva, who has received that gift from God.'

The secret of this was, that back of the suavity, giving it breadth and depth and truth, lay the tenderest and kindliest humanity. Here was a man at all points tempted as we are, whose own struggles and victories and even more, failures, give him infinite charity for the failures of others. There is never anywhere in Saint Francis tolerance of sin; but there is an inexhaustible tolerance and patience and sympathy for sinners.

And there is further, what one surely does not look for in a canonized saint, but what adds a fine flower to the saint's grace and charm, a rich and joyous gayety which sometimes broadens into laughter. In the 'Introduction to the Devout Life' Saint Francis, though reprehending all uncharitable mockery, permits and encourages light and kindly humor; and he himself does not hesitate to practice his own precept, even in his spiritual letters. 'Reverend mother, you should live before God in entire gayety of heart,' he writes to Madame de Chantal. And how winning is the gentle irony with which he dissuades an ardent novice from excess of devotion. 'My dear daughter, we must allow ourselves repose, enough repose; be kind enough to leave some labor to others, and not try to get all the crowns ourselves: our beloved neighbor will be charmed to have a few.'

This suavity, this charity, this large humanity, together with boundless tact and grace in handling souls, made Saint Francis probably one of the most skillful and successful spiritual directors that the Catholic Church has ever known, and it is in this aspect of his activity that the study of him is most interesting and most profitable. As to the value of such direction there has always been dispute and there always will be. Its dangers are obvious. No human soul can wholly take the burden of another. Yet every human soul has moments when it craves all the guidance and comfort that another soul can give it. Few have understood better than Saint Francis how to take advantage of these moments and make the comfort and the guidance lasting.

How far he influenced and governed men I cannot tell. His letters to them, except those of pure business or courtesy, are comparatively few. I cannot help thinking that some rebuff from the sterner sex occasioned one of his very rare expressions of discouragement: 'It is wonderful what power the fashions of this world have over mankind, and it seems hopeless to try to remedy this. If you hold up to them hell and damnation, they hide behind the goodness of God. If you press them, they leave you right where you stand.' Now and then he writes to some young nobleman, urging upon him the care of his soul. One answers, like Calchas in 'La Belle Hélène,' that his natural vocation is to enjoy himself. Ah, says the saint, listen to me and virtue will become a second nature stronger than the first. I wonder if the young man listened. To another Francis represents the value of the right use of time, and that some portion of the day at least should be given to prayer and meditation; at any rate, none to reading the fashionable follies of the hour, such as 'that infamous Rabelais.' And we are reminded of Valentin, the young friend of Goncourt. 'Valentin had only two books: a Bible of which he read a little every morning, a Rabelais, of which he read a little every night.' With all this, however, it must be remembered that our saint had the infinite respect of men of all classes and characters and that not a few of them came to him in trouble and sorrow and were comforted.

But unquestionably it was women who most often sought help and obtained it. As to his personal relations with them, it is hardly necessary to say that no word of reproach or suspicion is possible. His affection for Madame de Chantal was as pure as it was lofty. Their correspondence, carried on for many years, is one of the most beautiful examples of a spiritual relation mutually elevating, sustaining, and inspiring. With women generally he is said to have urged and to have himself practiced the most scrupulous regard for propriety and reserve, making it a rule never to speak to any woman except with a third person present in the room. Also he sets, perhaps half humorously, a rigorous prescription for letters: 'When one writes to a woman one ought, if it were possible, to use the point of a penknife, instead of a pen, so as to be sure to say nothing superfluous.' Although, as Sainte-Beuve, who quotes this, points out, with his usual charming naïveté he often forgets his own precept and wanders where it takes a swift and current pen to follow him.

In all his counsels to women it is interesting to note not only the high and stimulating impulse to spiritual intensity, but also the delicate restraining hand where spiritual intensity might be carried to excess. No one is more eager than he to urge the religious life upon those who are fit for it, ready for it. To a young girl whose parents are persuading her to marry for the sake of marriage, he says: 'Those who are naturally inclined to marry and are married happily find so much occasion for patience and for self-denial that they can hardly bear the burden; how should you bear it, when you have entered it against your will?' Yet in other cases he points out that the parent's wish should be thought of first, that domestic duties have their claim, and that a mother's love, although it sometimes seems tormenting, should be considered and respected before everything but the command of God.

Even to small matters of feminine frivolity he brings an affectionate touch of common sense. It is a pity to dress too daintily, but it is better to dress daintily than to worry about dressing daintily. 'Tell her to powder her hair, if she likes, so long as her heart is right; for the thing is not worth so much thinking about. Don't get your thoughts entangled among these spider-webs. The hairs of this girl's spirit are more snarled up than those of her head.' And although no one knows better than he the depth and power and richness of a woman's soul, there are times when he feels called upon to insist upon her weakness to an extent that would make the new woman somewhat restless. 'Your

352

sex needs to be led, and never succeeds in any en-
terprise but by submission; not that you have not
oftentimes as much light as men, but such is the
will of God.'

It is already sufficiently evident what fine observation, what delicate insight, what acute comparison and distinction were needed to practice the
art of soul-direction as Saint Francis practiced it.
Everywhere through his writings are scattered reflections and comments as subtle as those of La
Rochefoucauld or La Bruyère, the profound wisdom of a man who has walked through this cruel
and bitter world with eyes well open and not always turned upward. 'Everybody finds it easy to
practice certain virtues and hard to practice others,
and everybody exalts the virtue which he can practice easily and seeks to exaggerate the difficulty of
the virtues which are difficult to him.' Of the obstinate and stiff-necked he says: 'Thus we see that
it is a natural thing to be dominated by one's
opinions: melancholy persons are ordinarily much
more attached to them than those who are of a gay
and jovial disposition; for the latter are easily
turned by a light finger and ready to believe whatever is told them.' And the following shows with
what a quick, sharp probe he went right to the

bottom of a tormenting spiritual malady as haunting to-day as three hundred years ago. 'Mark these four words that I am going to say to you: your trouble comes from your fearing vice more than you love virtue. If you could give your soul from the very roots to the desire for practical religion, for loving-kindness, and for true humility, you would soon be an acceptable Christian, but you must think of these things all the time.'

Mere insight, however, would have carried the saint but little way in his spiritual labors. Far more important was his sympathy, his power of putting himself in others' places, his infinite love. There is nothing of remote austerity about him, nothing of judicial coldness. He never hesitates to admit his own frailty, his own temptation, his own failures. Has his patient — for what is he but a physician of the soul? — the disease of restlessness? He too has known the evil. 'May it not perhaps be a multitude of desires that obstructs your spirit? I myself have been ill of this malady. The bird tied to its perch knows itself to be bound and feels the shock of its detention only when it essays to fly away.' Or, as the 'Imitation' expresses it, with its inimitable and untranslatable grace, *Cella continuata dulcescit, sed male custodita tædium generat.* And what can be more charming than his confession, after years of ecclesiastical dignity, of the momentary specter, the intrusive and quickly banished shadow of human regret? 'Alas, my daughter, shall I tell you what happened to me the other day? Never in my life before have I had a single hint of temptation against my devout calling. But the other day, when I was least looking for it, such a thing came into my mind, not the wish that I did not belong to the Church, that would have been too gross; but because just before, talking with an intimate friend, I had said that if I were still free and were to become heir to a duchy, I should nevertheless choose the ecclesiastical profession, I loved it so much, a little debate arose in my soul, of should I or should I not, which lasted quite a space of time. I could see it, it seemed to me, way, way down in the baser portion of my soul, swelling like a toad. I laughed at it and would not even think whether I was thinking of it. So it went away in smoke and I saw it no more.' Would not you and I, who have our own toads crouching in dark corners, if we were to have a confessor at all, wish for a confessor like that?

So, on such a foundation of vast understanding and human sympathy, Saint Francis built up a method of spiritual direction which was all compact of charity and tenderness. For high and low alike he had the same breadth of comprehension, allowed for their failings and appreciated their difficulties. Rare indeed in the seventeenth century is the humanity which would deprive the rich of their pleasures out of regard for the poor. 'It is not reasonable that anybody should take his recreation at the expense of any one else, and especially by injuring the poor peasant, who is sufficiently oppressed at all times and whose labor and miserable condition we should always respect.' Everywhere in Saint Francis' writings there is the same consideration for weakness and wretchedness, the same desire to make the world better by pity rather than by scorn. Even where scorn is necessary, it should be restrained and moderated. Some things should be treated with contempt, 'but the contempt should be subdued and serious, not mocking nor full of disdain.'

But let us look more nearly at some aspects of Saint Francis' spiritual labors. To begin with, he was essentially practical, at times almost homely, did not by any means overstress meditation or pure devotion at the expense of everyday virtue. He insists usually upon truth with the strictest emphasis. 'I am comforted,' he says, in his quaint phraseology, 'to find that you have a horror of all finesse and duplicity; for there is no vice more contrary to the *embonpoint* and grace of the soul.' It is true he permits rare and professional exceptions. 'If anybody asks you whether you have told something that you have told under the sacred seal of confession, you may assert boldly, and with no fear of duplicity, that you have not.' But, in general, he stands as firm for entire truthfulness as any teacher of any age or country.

On the practice of little virtues he is charming. Not all can be saints, not all can teach or preach, not all can attain that glory which is perhaps as much of a false allurement in the things of virtue as in the things of vice. But there is plenty that all can do. 'More than any others, I love these three little virtues, gentleness of heart, poverty of spirit, simplicity of life; also these common deeds of charity, visiting the sick, aiding the poor, comforting the afflicted, and the like. But do these things without feverish anxiety and in the true freedom of the spirit.'

It is on this freedom of the spirit that he insists as much as upon anything. Do not fret, do not be anxious, do not be falsely careful. The service of

God is a joyous service. Over and over again he repeats these admonitions, which, with Madame de
Chantal, were apparently very needful. Now he
uses a homely vivacity of phrase which recalls Montaigne: 'Heavens, daughter, I wish the skin of your
heart were tougher, that the fleas might not keep
you waking.' Now he speaks with a grave tenderness which must have brought comfort to many a
weary sinner. 'We ought to hate our faults, but
with a hatred which should be quiet and tranquil,
not spiteful and full of restlessness.' Now his joyous fancy sings out in a burst of good cheer, the
delicate melody of which is quite untranslatable:
'*Laissez courir le vent et ne pensez pas que le frifilis
des feuilles soit le cliquetis des armes.*'

It seems hardly necessary to point out that these
practical matters are not all, or even the essential
part, of Saint Francis' teaching. Through his letters, through his sermons, through his treatises,
everywhere, runs the passionate insistence upon the
joy of spiritual rapture, upon the splendor, the
perfection, the all-absorbing ecstasy of communion
with God. It does not appear that Saint Theresa
herself felt this more fully or proclaimed it more
frequently. Only here, as always, Saint Francis
shows his serene common sense. Ecstasy is much,

he urges, but in our human life on this dusty earth it cannot be all. There are common duties from the performance of which no ecstasy can set us free. 'If it pleases God to let us taste of these angelic experiences, we will do out best to receive them worthily; meantime, let us devote ourselves simply and humbly to the little virtues which our Lord has commended to our effort and care.'

And as there are times when the sweetest and purest souls cannot rise above themselves, cannot shake off the dust of earth, are overcome and overwhelmed by shadow and despair, or by that dead inertia which is almost worse than despair, for these times especially Saint Francis is ready with consolation, ready with encouragement, ready with hope. Above all, he thinks, souls so cast down should not be chidden or reproved. Let them know, he urges all confessors, let them know that you too are human and have erred and suffered even as they. 'If, for example, you see one who is bowed down by remorse and shame, give him confidence and assurance that you are not an angel any more than he, that you find it in no way wonderful that a mere man should sin.' For those hours of wayward depression, which come without cause and vanish without warning, he has his own grace of tender reassurance. Do not strive too much, do not battle too much. Wait and hope and pray patiently for the goodness of God. And he analyzes such dark phases with a subtlety which shows that he knew well what he was talking about. 'The evil sadness comes upon you like a hailstorm with an unlooked for change and a vast impetuosity of terror. It comes all at once and you know not whence it comes, for it has no foundation in reason; nay, when it has come, it hunts about everywhere for reasons to justify itself. But the sweet and fruitful sadness comes gently upon the soul, like a soft rain which moistens blessedly, bringing the warmth of consolation; and it comes not unheralded, but for a good and sufficient cause.'

The reader cannot but have noticed already that Francis was not only a saint, but a great writer, and as with other great writers, his manner of writing is most significantly characteristic of the man himself. To be sure, he maintains that a preacher should put aside all thought of mere expression, and modestly disclaims any literary effort on his own part. 'I make no pretense of being a writer; for the sluggishness of my wit and the circumstances of my life — make such a thing impossible for me.' Yet it is permitted to doubt, with Sainte-Beuve, whether so fine a master of words did not take some pleasure in the use of them. Moreover, while denying to the preacher the privilege of literary artifice, Francis enjoins upon him the most careful employment of literary art as an exquisite and powerful means of moving souls. The distinction is sometimes a little hard to draw. But in the following admirable passage he states it clearly: 'In a word, you should speak affectionately and devoutly, simply and candidly, and with a firm faith; you should be profoundly possessed by the doctrine you teach and by all that you wish to impress upon others. The greatest artifice of all is to have no artifice. . . . You may say what you please, but the heart speaks to the heart, while mere words reach the ears only.' Elsewhere he defends the use of figurative expression. 'One word should be said about similitudes, they have an incredible efficiency in illuminating the understanding and in touching the will. . . . Similitudes from little things, subtly applied, are of extreme utility.'

In thus justifying figures of speech, he was justifying himself, as he well knew. For his own style is simple, quaint, tender, at times lofty and solemn; but what distinguishes it most is the extraordinary richness of imaginative suggestion, of similes drawn from every phase of nature and human life. Flowers, doves, bees, he is never weary of ringing the changes on them. It might be thought, perhaps, that the reader would weary; but he does not. There is such constant freshness of handling, such variety of detail, such an unfailing sense of the spiritual bearing of all these symbols, that you rejoice in each new one blossoming amid doctrinal discussion, as if it were a delicate flower in a barren plain.

And it is to be noted that the charm of these poetical digressions does not come from exact observation. Saint Francis is no Keats, no Thoreau, to spend hours watching the balance of a bird on a wind-tossed spray. Sometimes you get the impression that he has forgotten even prayer in listening to an autumn wind, or has enjoyed a golden morning just for itself, as when he says of doves 'their plumage is always smooth and it does you good to see them in the sunshine.' But generally his natural world — for that matter, like a good part of Shakespeare's, his exact contemporary — is taken from Pliny, from Virgil, from old books and quaint scholastics, from anything but God's blessed sky and the land and water under it. Phœnixes, unicorns, and salamanders play a large part in his menagerie, and his botany is too often in a class

362

with Falstaff's camomile: 'Honors, rank, dignities are like the saffron plant, which the more it is trodden on, the faster it grows.'

Yet genius and sincerity can make even wax flowers blossom, and Saint Francis draws from everything profit and help and comfort for the souls whose guidance is, after all, his great and only care. What a light, what a charm, what a winning, winged grace attaches to his words, when he speaks of 'marks of the love of God, signs of his good pleasure in our souls. *He nests in the hawthorne of our hearts.*'

What strikes me very much in the life and work of Saint Francis is the immense opportunity for the psychologist. One who has come to consider that nothing is so widely curious, so inexhaustibly fascinating as the study of the human soul, grows almost envious of such a field of purely scientific investigation. When the saint writes, 'I have met several souls, which, *closely examined*, offered nothing that I could consider sin,' what psychologist in his laboratory can often feel that souls have been *closely examined* in such a sense as that?

But great as the delight of such examination would be, it is easy to see how the saint could find a delight much greater. Indeed, he himself condemns the scientific pleasure of the psychologist as dangerous, if not impious. 'Many indulge in rash judgments for the pleasure of philosophizing and divining the characters of people as a mere intellectual exercise. If, by chance, they manage to hit the truth, their audacity and appetite for more increase so much, that it is almost impossible to turn them from the pursuit.'

In some of us the appetite and the audacity increase forever. But Saint Francis had interests even more absorbing. With him the object was not to know souls merely, but to help souls, to save souls. The direction of souls to him is 'the art of arts.' And who will differ from him? Simply to watch, to divine the play of secret springs in the inner life, is exquisite enough, but to use one's cunning sapience to mould souls as if they were wax, to bring light out of darkness, joy out of bitterness, comfort out of great trouble, and a pure and perfect flower out of what seemed a mass of corruption, could any human triumph be greater than this?

1913

THE END

APPENDIX

APPENDIX

SUGGESTIONS FOR A CLOSER ACQUAINTANCE WITH SAINTE-BEUVE

THERE are various references in this book to Sainte-Beuve as the master of all psychographers. The vast extent of Sainte-Beuve's work, sixty volumes, for the most part composed of disconnected articles heaped together by the varying exigencies of journalism, make it difficult for the casual reader to know how to approach him. It may therefore be worth while to offer a classified selection of a few of his most important studies, with indication of the volumes in which they are to be found.

PRINCIPAL WORKS OF SAINTE-BEUVE, WITH THE ABBREVIATIONS USED IN REFERRING TO THEM

Causeries du Lundi, fifteen volumes	*C. L.*
Nouveaux Lundis, thirteen volumes	*N. L.*
Portraits Contemporains, five volumes	*P. C.*
Portraits Littéraires, three volumes	*P. L.*

French History

Louis XIV	*C. L.*, V — *N. L.*, II.
Napoléon	*N. L.*, III.
Talleyrand	*N. L.*, XII.
Fouquet	*C. L.*, V.
Mirabeau	*C. L.*, IV.
Cardinal de Retz	*C. L.*, V.
Froissart	*C. L.*, IX.
Saint-Simon	*C. L.*, XV.

French Literature

Rabelais	*C. L.*, III.
Voltaire	*C. L.*, VII.
Rousseau	*C. L.*, III.
La Fontaine	*C. L.*, VII.
Joubert	*C. L.*, I.
George Sand	*C. L.*, I.

367

APPENDIX

The *Portraits Littéraires* contain various studies of the chief French literary figures of the classical period, and the *Portraits Contemporains* of Sainte-Beuve's contemporaries; but these are not his best or most significant work. The great history of *Port Royal*, in seven volumes, has much of extreme literary interest, notably the portrayal of Montaigne in the second volume.

Classics

This includes Sainte-Beuve's most delightful critical work.

Theocritus	*P. L.*, III.
Terence	*N. L.*, V.
Le Roman dans L'Antiquité	*N. L.*, II.
Pliny the Naturalist	*C. L.*, II.
Daphnis and Chloe	*N. L.*, IV.
The Greek Anthology	*N. L.*, VII.
Meleager	*P. C.*, V.
The Medea of Apollonius	*P. C.*, V.

The volume wholly devoted to Virgil is not among Sainte-Beuve's best.

English and Other Modern Literature

Franklin	*C. L.*, VII.
Gibbon	*C. L.*, VIII.
Cowper	*C. L.*, XI.
Lord Chesterfield	*C. L.*, II.
Don Quixote	*N. L.*, VIII.
Goethe	*C. L.*, XI.
Goethe and Bettina	*C. L.*, II.
Goethe and Eckermann	*N. L.*, III.
Frederic the Great	*C. L.*, III, *C. L.*, VII.

Religion

Saint-Anselme	*C. L.*, VI.
Saint François de Sales	*C. L.*, VII.
Fénelon	*C. L.*, II, *C. L.*, X.
Pascal	*C. L.*, V.
Bossuet	*C. L.*, X.
Saint-Martin	*C. L.*, X.
Eugénie de Guérin	*C. L.*, XII.

The seven volumes of *Port Royal* are also a mine of religious material.

APPENDIX

Women

Marie Antoinette	*C. L.*, IV.
Marie Stuart	*C. L.*, IV.
Mademoiselle de L'Espinasse	*C. L.*, II.
Madame de La Tour Franqueville	*C. L.*, II.
Madame de Grafigny	*C. L.*, II.
Madame Du Châtelet	*C. L.*, II.
Madame Geoffrin	*C. L.*, II.
La Duchesse Du Maine	*C. L.*, III.
La Comtesse d'Albany	*N. L.*, V.
La Comtesse de Boufflers	*N. L.*, IV.
Madame de Verdelin	*N. L.*, IX.

If one were to pick out any one representative volume of Sainte-Beuve, one could not do better than take Volume II of the *Causeries du Lundi*, made up largely of the above portraits of women. The *Portraits de Femmes* is mainly earlier and inferior work.

Subjects of little note in themselves but rendered profoundly interesting by Sainte-Beuve's treatment:

Saint-Évremond	*C. L.*, IV.
Huet	*C. L.*, II.
Sismondi	*N. L.*, VI.
Maurice de Guérin	*C. L.*, XV.
Boissonade	*N. L.*, VI.
Ducis	*N. L.*, IV.